*Mary,*
*Thank you for the countless ways that you foster discipleship of heart and mind! Thank you as well for your encouragement and support of the C.S. Lewis Institute!*
*Gratefully,*
*Joel*

# DISCIPLESHIP WITH C.S. LEWIS

A Guide to *Mere Christianity* for Small Groups
and Mentoring Relationships

*Philippians 1: 3-6*

JOEL WOODRUFF

*Joel Woodruff*

*Discipleship with C.S. Lewis* is the result of an inspired idea: use C.S. Lewis's *Mere Christianity*, a series of radio talks delivered to the British nation during the Second World War, as the basis for disciple-making today. The ongoing war in heaven continues to spill over onto earth as various forces, including social media, compete for the hearts and minds of men and women, young or old. The first task is to identify the enemy, and this is what Woodruff ably does – with a little help from Lewis. The larger task is to train people to live out their faith in the God of the gospel, and this involves conforming one's beliefs and behavior to the reality of Jesus Christ, the revelation of God and the exemplar of humanity. *Discipleship with C.S. Lewis* is not only a Christian call to arms, but a training manual for preparing Christians to be battle-ready.

-Dr. Kevin J. Vanhoozer, Research Professor of Systematic Theology, Trinity Evangelical Divinity School

Most people perceive C.S. Lewis's *Mere Christianity* to be an apologetics book. But Joel Woodruff demonstrates that this most influential work is fundamentally about discipleship, touching heart and mind. He has put together an invaluable training manual to accompany Lewis's book, utilizing biblical texts, summaries, key questions to ponder, and action steps to incorporate into one's life. An ideal tool for both personal discipleship and group settings.

-Dr. Dennis P. Hollinger, President Emeritus & Senior Distinguished Professor of Christian Ethics, Gordon-Conwell Theological Seminary

Jesus Christ commissioned His church to make disciples. Dr. Joel Woodruff's splendid book reveals how C.S. Lewis's classic *Mere Christianity* can be employed as a training manual for Christian spiritual formation and fulfilling the Great Commission.

-Dr. Lyle Dorsett, C.S. Lewis Scholar,
Former Billy Graham Professor of Evangelism
at Samford University's Beeson Divinity School

As a pastor, I am always looking for tools to help foster discipling relationships for spiritual formation. Used in conjunction with the Bible, Lewis's *Mere Christianity* offers a stimulating resource for Christian belief, character, and practice. Joel's book, *Discipleship with C.S. Lewis,* provides a user-friendly guide, and I look forward to using it in our church to get people pursuing Christian growth together.

-Dr. Bill Kynes, Pastor,
Cornerstone Evangelical Free Church, Annandale, VA

Joel's excellent user-friendly book not only enables one to grasp and apply the essential truths of Lewis's *Mere Christianity*, it provides a pathway for ongoing healthy discipleship. His multi-faceted approach of foundational biblical passages, insight-provoking questions, specific action steps, Scripture memory and perceptive conclusions will help build a community of loving and discerning disciples.

-Steve King, Senior Pastor Emeritus,
Cherrydale Baptist Church, Arlington VA

Countless readers have been brought to faith in Christ through the brilliance of *Mere Christianity* and still today, skeptics are seeing Lewis's own spiritual journey lead them on a similar pathway toward Jesus. *Discipleship with C.S. Lewis* takes this process and helps believers engage both the heart and the mind in discipleship, building up their spiritual senses and strengthening their theological commitments. I heartily recommend this book written and presented beautifully by Joel Woodruff. If you are serious about discipleship, you will want to have this book as a resource for personal or group study.

-Daniel Darling, Vice-President of Communications, The Ethics and Religious Liberty Commission

In his excellent book, Dr. Joel Woodruff leads the reader through a robust and practical engagement with the content of C.S. Lewis's *Mere Christianity*. But he also goes one step further – he opens the path for the reader to grapple with the very Scriptures which so deeply shaped and infused Lewis's thought. The result is material that I would heartily recommend to any desiring a deeper discipleship.

-Connally Gilliam, Author of *Revelations of a Single Woman*, U.S. Navigators Staff

Many of us love C. S. Lewis's *Mere Christianity*. We recommend it, give away copies of it, and occasionally quote it. But we may have never employed it as a discipleship tool. Joel Woodruff's keen eye as an educator, equips us do just that. He helps us explore Lewis's masterpiece reflectively, ponder it theologically, and apply it penetratingly. I highly recommend this work.

-Dr. Randy Newman,
Senior Teaching Fellow for Apologetics and Evangelism,
The C. S. Lewis Institute

*Mere Christianity* remains essential reading for any who want to engage in a robust grasp of the faith. Since the perennial questions are asked generation after generation, Lewis, for his clarity and precision remains as relevant today as he was 75 years ago when these presentations were given on the BBC Radio in England during World War II. Furthermore, in an age so polarized, Lewis models intellectual rigor without rancor. His charity comes through in all he writes. Joel Woodruff's *Discipleship with C.S. Lewis* is a must for any desiring to study *Mere Christianity* or lead groups through its invigorating topics. I recommend it with enthusiasm.

-Dr. Jerry Root, C. S. Lewis Scholar, Professor of Evangelism,
Wheaton College

## The Author

Joel Woodruff is the President of the C.S. Lewis Institute, a discipleship ministry of heart and mind with locations throughout the United States, Canada and Great Britain. He is passionate about seeing people grow in their love for Jesus Christ and become faithful disciple-makers. He has worked in higher education, non-profit administration, and pastoral ministries in Alaska, Israel, Hungary, France, and Washington, D.C. He is a graduate of Wheaton College, and Gordon-Conwell Theological Seminary and holds a doctorate from Nova Southeastern University. He and his wife Dolly and their children live in Northern Virginia.

# DISCIPLESHIP WITH C.S. LEWIS

A Guide to *Mere Christianity* for Small Groups
and Mentoring Relationships

**Leaders Guide Included**

**21 Studies Using the Bible and *Mere Christianity***

**Perfect for Small Groups**

CSLI
PRESS

JOEL WOODRUFF

Discipleship with C.S. Lewis: A Guide to *Mere Christianity*
for Small Groups and Mentoring Relationships

Published by CSLI Press
8001 Braddock Road, Suite 301
Springfield, VA 22151

Unless otherwise indicated, all Scripture quotations are from The Holy Bible, English Standard Version® (ESV®), copyright © 2001 by Crossway Bibles, a publishing ministry of Good News Publishers. Used by permission. All rights reserved.

 ISBN 978-1-54399-523-7 eBook 978-1-54399-524-4

# ACKNOWLEDGEMENTS

I thank God for placing godly men and women in my life to disciple me over the years to help me grow in my faith in and love for Jesus Christ. Some of these saints have since entered glory including my parents Steve and Joanne Woodruff, my grandparents Al and Data May Woodruff, my grandmother Esther Spicher, my father- and mother-in-law Paul and Mimi Riegert, tennis coach Kiah Evans, the athletic director of Wheaton College Jack Swartz, and a praying seminary professor Christy Wilson.

Although he died the year that I was born, I thank God for C.S. Lewis as this book would not have been possible without his life, faith, and writings.

I'm blessed to have living disciple-makers in my life including the pastor of my youth Jerry Hilton, my former boss Bob McIntyre, my aunt Margaret King, and the past and current leaders of the C.S. Lewis Institute including Jim Hiskey, Jim Houston, Art Lindsley, Tom Tarrants, Kerry Knott and Tom Simmons. My prayer is that this book reflects the wisdom and love that all of these disciples of Jesus Christ have passed on to me.

I'm also grateful to God for my brothers, Jon and Jeremy Woodruff, and cousin, Kevin King, who have been examples to me and encouraged me to stand for Jesus daily.

A special note of thanks goes to Ed Glancy and Evelyn Bence for their editorial skills, Crystal Sarno for her design ideas and Semy Godo and Jake Fritzke at the C.S. Lewis Institute.

# DEDICATIONS

This book is dedicated to my beautiful wife, Dolly, who by God's grace, has served alongside me in seeking to follow Jesus Christ, and to my children, Noah, Idan, Gloria and Esther in the hope that as passionate disciples of our Lord they will articulate, defend, share and live their faith in personal and public life.

# CONTENTS

## Part 3: An Introduction to Christian Theology and Discipleship

## Appendices

# INTRODUCTION

## Why *Mere Christianity* as a Discipleship Training Manual?

As bombs were falling on London, and the air Battle for Britain was being waged between the German Luftwaffe and the Royal Air Force, the British people again confronted the horrors of war. Prime Minister Winston Churchill took to the microphone and via radio inspired his nation to fight valiantly against Hitler's forces to preserve all that they knew to be good and true. Even so, the British government knew that the destruction, death, and sorrow of World War II were taking its toll on the morale of its people. The nation needed some spiritual encouragement. War tends to surface the deeper questions of life and God, questions that can lead to despondency or hope. So the search was on: who could provide real answers in a compelling fashion to the spiritual questions of a nation? The directors of the British Broadcasting Corporation (BBC) turned to an Oxford literature professor by the name of Clive Staples Lewis, better known as C.S. Lewis.

Lewis soon became the second-best-known radio voice on the BBC, after Churchill. Lewis's broadcast talks gave hope to the British people as he shared spiritual insights in a down-to-earth way. He had served as an infantry officer in World War I, been wounded, and knew the nightmares of war firsthand. Wartime caused him to struggle with the meaning of life. He had deep spiritual questions; for more than a decade after the First World War, he explored the worldviews of various philosophies, atheism,

Hinduism, Islam, Judaism, and finally came to the conclusion that Jesus Christ provided the most rational and fulfilling answers to the spiritual questions of life. His personal experiences, sharp intellect, understanding of philosophy, religion and the classics, his Irish gift of storytelling, his love for God and the people of his nation enabled him to passionately use these radio broadcasts (1942-1944) to share with listeners of all classes and backgrounds the essentials of "Mere Christianity."

These radio broadcasts, now known in book form as *Mere Christianity*, were shaped in the midst of wartime. Lewis knew that war sharpens our focus on the ultimate realities of life. Whether one's nation is at war or not, Lewis noted that the Christian life is lived in "enemy-occupied territory" and that disciples of Jesus are engaged in a battle with the world, the flesh, and the devil. For this reason, *Mere Christianity* identifies the enemies to faith in Jesus Christ, gives a rational defense for Christianity, and pro-vides disciples with basic training in the beliefs, behaviors, and disciplines of the Christian life that will help them stand strong in battle. Lewis took Jesus Christ and His commands seriously as a soldier would take the orders of his regimental commander. Thus *Mere Christianity*, while it has been used often as an apologetics and evangelistic tool, is at its core a discipleship training manual for followers of Jesus Christ.

It is a handbook that can be used in "boot camp" or in the midst of battle for equipping both the new and experienced disciple to become a reproducing, wholehearted follower of Jesus Christ.

If Lewis were alive today, he would be surprised to learn that *Mere Christianity* was named the most influential Christian book of the twentieth century by *Christianity Today* magazine. This reflects the book's effectiveness in presenting the essence of Christianity to millions of people since its publication in 1952. Many have come to faith in Christ by reading its well-reasoned arguments for the Christian faith. A number of resources have helped people explore the apologetics arguments of the book. Others have analyzed the book by taking a more academic or philosophic approach. As a result, some people think *Mere Christianity* is only about apologetics or too heady or difficult to navigate except by "intellectuals." This is unfortunate because, although there is an intellectual piece to the book, especially in the philosophically oriented first section, Book 1, most of it is down to earth and very practical. Its orientation is toward discipleship, so that Christians can articulate, defend, share, and live their faith in Christ joyfully in all aspects of life.

This study of *Mere Christianity*, as opposed to more academic or apologetics-oriented studies, is written with a view toward practical Christian discipleship of heart and mind. It will help participants develop an understanding of the biblical teachings behind the main themes within *Mere Christianity*. Participants will be encouraged to apply the takeaways in each session through concrete steps that influence their daily lives and help them become more faithful and fruitful disciples of Jesus. I believe that if C.S. Lewis were present with us today, he would take great pleasure knowing that God was using his World War II, BBC broadcasts to help develop spiritual warriors for Jesus Christ, prepared for battle–spreading the love and good news of Jesus in the midst of "enemy-occupied territory."

# HOW BEST TO USE: DISCIPLESHIP WITH C.S. LEWIS: A GUIDE TO *MERE CHRISTIANITY* FOR SMALL GROUPS AND MENTORING RELATIONSHIPS

## Books Needed:

*The Bible*, preferably a good study Bible.

*Mere Christianity*, by C.S. Lewis

**Purpose:** To train disciples of Jesus by using *Mere Christianity* as a discipleship training manual alongside key biblical passages to establish a firm foundation for Christian belief, character, and practice. As a discipleship course, both new and experienced followers of Jesus will discover the reasonableness and power of the Christian faith, especially as it is shared and lived out in our contemporary world. Ultimately it is hoped that participants will grow in their faith, deepen their relationship with Jesus, and become more faithful and fruitful followers of Christ as they allow the Holy Spirit to instruct them through this study.

**One comprehensive study or three shorter yet complete studies:** Each of the three parts to this study (Christian Beliefs; Christian Behavior; and An Introduction to Christian Theology and Discipleship) can be used as a separate study in and of itself. But the full three-part discipleship course provides a more complete initial grounding in essentials of the Christian faith.

**One-on-one or small-group approach:** This study is designed for one-on-one or small-group study. In a one-on-one approach,

I suggest that an experienced follower of Christ walk through this study with a person newer to the faith. This would allow open discussion of questions that may arise.

Another method would be for a more mature Christian to take two or three others through the study together. This allows for a wider range of questions and discussion as each person contributes a unique perspective. It also can provide energy to group dynamics.

Small groups could also use this study, with one ongoing facilitator or a leadership that rotates among group participants.

Each session includes the study of one or more biblical passages and readings from *Mere Christianity*. I suggest that each person do the readings privately and write out answers to the questions before meeting together. The questions and answers can be used as a guide for discussion of the material.

I encourage groups to begin and close the discussion time in prayer, asking God to reveal His truth. The study will be more effective if each person writes down at least one action point to work on in the coming week. For example, if the study is about the Golden Rule, participants would find a concrete, intentional way to do something for someone else that they would like to have done for themselves.

**Facilitator/Leadership Guide:** A brief facilitator/leadership guide can be found in the Appendices.

**How *Mere Christianity* is used in this study:** *Mere Christianity* is divided into four books that reflect to some degree the order in which Lewis delivered his BBC radio broadcasts over the course of several years.

This study will begin with book 2, titled "What Christians Believe." Here Lewis outlines in an engaging manner the foundational teachings of "Mere Christianity" that come out of the apostles' teaching from the Bible and are summarized in the Apostles' Creed. Appendix 1 includes the Apostles' Creed as a reference.

The second part of this study will examine book 3, "Christian Behaviour," in which Lewis examines the means by which the Christian is to live out personal beliefs in thought, word, and deed. This includes a look at how a person relates to God, to others, and to oneself. Christian wisdom, goodness, sexual morality, marriage, humility, forgiveness, faith, hope, and love are discussed.

The third part of this study examines book 4, "Beyond Personality: Or First Steps in the Doctrine of the Trinity." Lewis gives the believer some basic lessons in Christian discipleship and offers some thoughts on several theological questions and concepts.

Appendix 2 includes an optional study of Lewis's book 1, titled "Right and Wrong as a Clue to the Meaning of the Universe." This book is more philosophical in nature and provides a foundation for the idea that morality—the concept of right and wrong—points to a moral Creator. This important book is summarized briefly in book 2—the reason for book 1 not being covered in the body of the study.

This study assigns readings using the book number and the chapter number of the reading from *Mere Christianity*. This enables use of any edition of *Mere Christianity*. Any *Mere Christianity* quotation in a specific session is from the book and chapter under discussion.

**How the Bible is used in this study:** This study selects biblical passages that address the key themes of Christian belief and practice discussed in *Mere Christianity*. C.S. Lewis believed in the authority of the Bible as God's Word revealed to humankind. He once wrote to a friend, "What we are committed to believing is whatever can be proved from Scripture."[1]

Thus Lewis would want the reader to study the Bible as the ultimate means of learning and applying God's truth to our lives. Participants in this study are encouraged to study the Bible and find other passages that would deepen and highlight the truths discussed in *Mere Christianity*.

**Summary for each session:** Each study session includes some "Concluding Observations" on the key points addressed in both the Bible passage and the writing of C.S. Lewis. This section can be used as a means of outlining and reviewing what you've studied.

**Bible memory verse(s) for each session:** Each study session closes with a suggested Bible memory passage. By taking time to memorize these verses, God's Word will be stored in your mind and heart. One way to memorize is to write out the verses on note cards or sticky notes. Place these in places frequented throughout the day (the bathroom mirror, car dashboard, office wall, etc.). By repeating one verse over the course of a week and chewing on it (meditating on it), you will come to understand it more deeply. Repeat passages out loud as you start your discussion time together. This study uses the English Standard Version, but you may use any preferred version for memorization.

---

1. C.S. Lewis, 1945 letter to Lyman Stebbins, quoted in James Como, "C.S. Lewis' Quantum Church: An Uneasy Meditation," in *C.S. Lewis and the Church: Essays in Honour of Walter Hooper*, ed. Judith Wolfe and Brendan N. Wolfe (London: Bloomsbury, 2012), 98.

**For more on C.S. Lewis:** To learn more about the life and faith of C.S. Lewis, visit the website of the C.S. Lewis Institute: www. cslewisinstitute.org.

There you may download a free e-book on Lewis, *C.S. Lewis: A Profile in Faith.*

His spiritual autobiography, covering his childhood years through his conversion to Christianity as an adult, is titled *Surprised by Joy: The Shape of My Early Life.*

Once Lewis became a disciple of Jesus Christ, he used both reason and imagination to communicate his faith to others through a variety of books, including children's fiction (The Chronicles of Narnia), science fiction (The Space Trilogy), and Christian works such as *Miracles, The Problem of Pain*, and *Mere Christianity.*

Lewis died on November 20, 1963, the same day that John F. Kennedy was assassinated. Lewis thought he'd be forgotten as an author within a few years after his death. He would be surprised to know that he is better known as an author today than ever before. His books continue to sell millions of copies each year, and a number of his fiction works have been turned into movies and dramatic productions on Broadway. His life story has also been the subject of numerous books, movies, and academic works.

## PART I: CHRISTIAN BELIEFS

A Study of Book 2 of *Mere Christianity*:
"What Christians Believe"

# SESSION 1-1

## Rival Understandings of God

> Atheism turns out to be too simple. If the whole universe has no meaning, we should never have found out that it has no meaning: just as, if there were no light in the universe and therefore no creatures with eyes, we should never know it was dark. **Dark** would be a word without meaning.
>
> –C.S. Lewis, *Mere Christianity*, *book 2, chapter 1*

## Questions to Explore

1. Does God exist?

2. If God exists, what is God like?

3. If a good God made the world, why has it gone so wrong?

4. How does the idea of justice (some things are just and others unjust) refute the atheist's idea that life as we know it is the result of random chance?

## Preparation for Session

On your own, read the following Bible study passage and chapter in *Mere Christianity*. Write answers to the accompanying questions to use in your upcoming discipleship discussion of the themes, truths, and ideas being presented. To love and serve those in your study meeting, come prepared to actively discuss what you've discovered, listen to the insights of others, and pray for one another. Ask the Holy Spirit to guide and teach you as you seek to know truth and live it out. Remember that you are living in "enemy-occupied territory," so be aware of potential distractions or temptations that might potentially hinder your spiritual growth. Be faithful, available, and teachable so that you can become a more effective disciple of Jesus Christ. Follow this same approach for each subsequent session.

## Bible Study

Read Genesis 1:1–2:3.

Genesis chronicles the creation of the world and humankind by God. It reveals clues to the nature of God, the meaning of life, and reality as we know it today on this earth. It provides an essential foundation to understanding the Christian faith. Answer the following questions based on your reading of Genesis 1:1–2:3:

1.  According to the Bible, does God exist? If so, what words are used to describe God? What is God like?

2.  What can you know about God from what God does?

3.  What can you know about God from what God says?

4.  How is God's creation described at creation intervals? What does this imply about the nature of God, the One who created the world?

5.  What is the relationship between matter—the created physical world—and God?

6. How are men and women described after they are created? What does this imply about their relationship to the Creator in comparison to the rest of creation?

## Study of *Mere Christianity*

Read book 2, "What Christians Believe," chapter 1, "The Rival Conceptions of God." Answer the following questions in response to your reading:

1. What is the first major division of humanity in regard to belief in God? Is this a correct observation of the world today? Why or why not?

2. Think of someone you know who is an atheist—a person who believes there is no God. How would this person support belief that the world is senseless, random, and without ultimate meaning?

3.   How did the ideas of just and unjust, right and wrong, eventually lead C.S. Lewis to believe that the atheistic viewpoint is too simple for explaining reality as we know it?

4.   How would you communicate to a friend in your own words the idea that just and unjust; right and wrong; fair and unfair are pointers to the existence of God?

5.   What is the second major division of humanity in regard to belief in God?

6.   Think of someone you know who is a pantheist—a person who believes that everything is God and that God is not different and separate from all created things including human beings (forms of Hinduism, Buddhism, or New Age spirituality). How do you think this person would defend belief that God is beyond good and evil? What are the implications of this belief?

7. What does the Christian idea of God say about God's relationship to the created world and to human beings? What are the implications of this?

8. What do the implications of the Christian idea of God—that God is good and not evil—have on our understanding of the world?

9. Lewis summarizes the Christian view of reality: "For Christianity is a fighting religion. It thinks God made the world – that space and time, heat and cold, and all the colours and tastes, and all the animals and vegetables, are things that God 'made up out of His head' as a man makes up a story. But it also thinks that a great many things have gone wrong with the world that God made and that God insists, and insists very loudly, on our putting them right again." Does Lewis's view of reality square with the biblical story as found in Genesis? Why or why not?

10. How would you state the Christian view of reality in your own words to a friend?

## Action Steps

1. If you believe God made the world, write down right now one action step that you could take each day in the coming week to acknowledge God as the One who created you and created this world. For instance, you could start a "thank-you note" to God and add to it each day. You might take a daily walk, observe the created world, and talk to God about it. Use your creativity and be intentional.

2. Commit to praying daily and asking God to show you His truth and wisdom.

## Bible Memory Verse

"In the beginning, God created the heavens and the earth" (Genesis 1:1).

## Concluding Observations on Genesis 1:1-2:3 and Book 2, Chapter 1 of *Mere Christianity*

When describing humanity as a whole, Lewis sees two primary divisions. The first is between the majority of humankind who believe in some kind of God or gods and the minority made up of materialists or atheists who do not believe in God. The second division is with regard to the kind of God or gods people believe in. Pantheists (Hindus, Buddhists, New Agers) believe God is beyond good and evil. They believe that the universe is God (everything is one) and is animated by God. God is impersonal to the pantheist. The goal is oneness that can come only when diversity and human individuality is eradicated into the great Oneness.

Monotheists (Jews, Christians, and Muslims) believe that God created the world and is separate from His creation. They believe that God is good and that the world, animals, plants, and human beings were created as good. Human beings are distinct from the rest of the creation; they are created in God's image. The Christian believes that something has gone wrong in the world in opposition to God and His goodness and that God is in the process of redeeming human beings and the world. This is the starting point for the Christian worldview.

One clue to the meaning of the universe is the understanding that we all have some knowledge of right and wrong, fair and unfair, just and unjust. Built into this understanding of right and wrong is the assumption that at least one part of reality—the concept of justice—is full of meaning. Thus the atheist who states the world is senseless or without meaning is caught flat-footed.

# SESSION 1-2

## The Problems of Sin, Satan, and Evil

*Enemy-occupied territory—that is what this world is. Christianity is the story of how the rightful king has landed, you might say landed in disguise, and is calling us all to take part in a great campaign of sabotage.*

–C.S. Lewis, *Mere Christianity,* book 2, chapter 2

## Questions to Explore

1. How do we explain the problem of evil?

2. Who is the devil, and what is he trying to accomplish in the world?

3. Why is the concept of spiritual warfare important to understanding reality?

4. What is God's response to evil?

## Bible Study

Read Genesis 2:4-3:24.

In Genesis 2 we learn that people are created for relationship with God and one another. Adam and Eve, the first man and woman, are designed to complement each other, to have offspring, to work in the Garden of Eden, and to care for it. They are given power and freewill to make decisions and choices on their own. For instance, they determine the names of the animals and all other living things. They are given one command by God, which they can choose to follow or disobey, "You may surely eat of every tree of the garden, but of the tree of the knowledge of good and evil you shall not eat, for in the day that you eat of it you shall surely die" (vv. 16-17). Adam and Eve at this stage in history are "naked and unashamed," indicating that they are in perfect relationship with God and one another.

In Genesis 3 we learn how evil, the devil (disguised as the serpent), and human sin enter the world. Answer the following questions based on your reading of Genesis 2:4-3:24:

1.    How does the serpent when speaking to the woman distort God's word in Genesis 2 and call into question the goodness of God?

2.    How do the created human beings rebel against their Creator? Why is their rebellion an affront to the goodness and justice of God?

3.    Why do Adam and Eve hide from God? What does this signify?

4.    How does God demonstrate that He is just yet also merciful in the way He deals with Adam and Eve?

5.    How does God deal with the devil/serpent? What is prophesied about the fate of the devil in Genesis 3:15? How does this give hope to humankind?

6.    How do we know that God, who is good, will defeat evil in the end?

7.    Describe in one to three sentences the relationships between God, humankind, and the devil in this post-Edenic world, the world as we know it after sin entered the world through Adam and Eve.

Read Revelation 12:7-17, which might be described as the fall of Satan, the devil. Then answer the following questions based on your reading:

1. Who is Satan?

2. How do the angels/demons that choose to rebel against God leave heaven?

3. What are Satan and his demons (fallen angels) doing on earth? What is their goal?

4. What is the final destiny of Satan and his demons according to Jesus?

## Study of *Mere Christianity*

Read book 2, chapter 2, "The Invasion," in *Mere Christianity*. Answer the following questions in response to your reading:

1. Why does the "Christianity-and-water" idea, or what we would call today "liberal Christianity" that leaves out the hard biblical teachings on sin, hell, the devil, and the cross, not hold up against reality?

2. Why is dualism, the idea that good and evil are two independent equals (i.e., Taoism, yin and yang) undermined by the concept of justice—that there really is an absolute standard of good?

3. Who is the devil, and what is he trying to do in the world?

4. Why is it important to be aware of the devil's work in the world?

5. Name some ways by which people make light of the devil.

6.   In the preface to *The Screwtape Letters,* C.S. Lewis wrote, "There are two equal and opposite errors into which our race can fall about the devils. One is to disbelieve in their existence. The other is to believe, and to feel an excessive and unhealthy interest in them. They themselves are equally pleased by both errors and hail a materialist or a magician with the same delight." Do you agree or disagree with Lewis's assessment? If you agree, how and where do you see the devil receiving too little or too much credit in the world today?

## Action Steps

1.   Write down right now at least one action step you could take to becoming more aware of—and thwarting—the evil in the world and in your own behavior. For example, you can plan ahead—if you catch yourself thinking evil thoughts about someone, you can act to change those thoughts, pray for the person, and ask God to help you exhibit love. Or if you have read of a horrific crime, such as sex trafficking, in the news, you could identify and financially support an organization that is fighting that evil.

2.   Commit to praying daily and asking God to show you His truth and wisdom.

## Bible Memory Verse

"Therefore, just as sin came into the world through one man, and death through sin, and so death spread to all men because all sinned" (Romans 5:12).

## Concluding Observations on Genesis 2:4–3:24, Revelation 12:7–17, and Book 2, Chapter 2 of *Mere Christianity*

The reality of evil in the world is difficult to explain. Atheism is too simple in that it denies the categories of good and evil. Liberal Christianity, what Lewis calls "Christianity-and-water," focuses on the goodness of God and writes off the devil, demons, hell, supernatural forces, miracles, and other hard teachings as old-school ideas that lack credibility in our modern, scientific understanding of the world. This view simplifies things with a naïve hope that somehow a good God will make everything right again without any consequences for evil in the world. It promotes God's love without understanding the holy love of God that needs to eradicate sin, evil, and hatred for true redemption to occur.

Dualism, the idea of two equal forces—one evil and one good—the Taoist view, fails to offer hope as in this schema God is not the ultimate victor; good will never triumph over evil.

True Christian faith, on the other hand, believes that God is good and any created beings in opposition to God are evil. These evil forces, however, are not equal to God and in fact are quite inferior to the awesome, holy, loving God who created the world. The devil is a real creature, a fallen angel in rebellion against God, who entered the Garden of Eden to tempt Adam and Eve and lead them away from God to join with him in rebellion against God

17

our Creator. When Adam and Eve chose to listen to the serpent (the devil) and disobey God's loving commands, they opened the door for sin and evil to enter the human sphere. The earth is now "enemy-occupied territory," as the devil, his demons, and sinful human beings wreak havoc, bringing about sin, suffering, and acts of evil. God in His goodness, however, has responded by sending His Son, Jesus, into the world to redeem it. Christians, those who have responded to the loving grace of God through Jesus for the forgiveness of their sins, are now fighting with God's help to stop the devil, his evil forces, and human sin and to share the good news of Christ that saves human beings from the lies and traps of this evil world and the devil.

# SESSION 1-3

## God's Response to Sin, Satan, and Evil

*Free will, though it makes evil possible, is also the only thing that makes possible any love or goodness or joy worth having. A world of automata—of creatures that worked like machines—would hardly be worth creating.*

*—C.S. Lewis, Mere Christianity, book 2, chap. 3*

## Questions to Explore:

1. Why did God create human beings with potential to sin and do evil?

2. How did the devil go wrong and steer human beings to do wrong?

3. Why have so many attempts to find meaning in life failed?

4. What did God give to human beings to recognize the problem of sin and give them signs of hope?

5. What is God's response to sin?

6.    Who does Jesus claim to be?

## Bible Study

Read Mark 2:1-12. Answer the following questions based on your reading:

1.    Why did people come to see Jesus?

2.    What did the friends of the paralytic man believe Jesus could do for their friend?

3.    What was Jesus' response to the faith of the friends of the paralytic man?

4.    Why were the scribes shocked by Jesus' statement, "Son, your sins are forgiven"?

5.    Who is Jesus clearly claiming to be by His words and actions?

6.  What is the response of the crowd to Jesus' healing of the paralytic man and His pronouncement that He had forgiven the man's sins?

7.  After reading this passage, do you believe Jesus' claims about Himself? Why or why not?

## Study of *Mere Christianity*

Read book 2, chapter 3, "The Shocking Alternative," in *Mere Christianity*. Answer the following questions in response to your reading:

1.  If God is good and has absolute power, how can anything happen that is contrary to His will?

2.  Why did God give human beings free will, the ability to choose between doing good or evil, if it makes evil choices possible?

3.  How did the "dark power," "the prince of this world," "the devil" or "Satan," go wrong?

4.  What sin did Satan teach the human race?

5.  What is the result of searching for happiness outside of God and His will?

6.  What is God's response to humankind's repetition of Satan's sin and evil?

7.  Some claim that Jesus was a great moral teacher but not God. Why is that possibility untenable based on Jesus' statements and beliefs about Himself?

8.  According to Lewis, Jesus leaves us with three options. He is a lunatic, a liar, or Lord. Some have added a fourth

category of a legend. Whom do you believe Jesus to be? Why is this perhaps the most important question of all?

## Action Steps

1. Write down ways in which you can actively thank and praise God for His response to evil through the life and work of Jesus.

2. Think about how you might share the good news about Jesus and what He has done for us with a friend or colleague. Write down some of your thoughts and continue to reflect upon how to communicate this to others.

3. Commit to praying daily and asking God to show you His truth and wisdom.

## Bible Memory Verse

"'But that you may know that the Son of Man has authority on earth to forgive sins'—he said to the paralytic—'I say to you, rise, pick up your bed, and go home.' And he rose and immediately picked up his bed and went out before them all, so that they were all amazed and glorified God, saying, 'We never saw anything like this!'" (Mark 2:10-12).

## Concluding Observations on Mark 2:1-12 and Book 2, Chapter 3 of *Mere Christianity*

The question many struggle with is this: If God is all-powerful and good, why would He create angels and human beings with the power to do both good and evil and thus allow sin, suffering, and evil to enter the world? Lewis argues that God created His higher creatures with the potential to voluntarily be united to Him. In other words, He gave humankind and angels free will to love God and one another. They are not machines without any control over their own destiny but, rather, beings able to experience the happiness and joy that comes from a mutually chosen loving relationship. The higher a creature is, the smarter, the freer, and the stronger it will be with the potential for great glory or great misery. Satan fell when he succumbed to the sin of pride, wanting to be greater than God and in control. He shared this sin with the human race. The end result is a lack of fulfillment and meaning in life. So people try all kinds of means to find happiness outside of a relationship with God. As Lewis explains, "Out of that hopeless attempt has come nearly all that we call human history—money, poverty, ambition, war, prostitution, classes, empires, slavery—the long terrible story of man trying to find something other than God which will make him happy."

By God's grace, He gave humans a conscience; they at least know that some things are good and others evil. This becomes apparent in all cultures, which share stories that point to God and a desire to be restored to life after death. God also initiated His rescue plan for humankind immediately after sin entered the world; then through the Hebrew nation, He prepared the world for its Savior—Jesus Christ, the Son of God. When Jesus entered His ministry as described in the Gospels, He claimed to be able to forgive sin, something only God could do. He proved this by exercising His supernatural powers in which He was able to heal disease, cast out demons, preach with authority, as well as proclaim words of forgiveness over people who put their faith in Him.

When considering the person of Jesus, men and women must determine whether He was a liar, a lunatic, a legend, or truly Lord—the all-powerful God of the universe come in human form to save us from our sin. He doesn't give us the choice of accepting Him as merely a great moral teacher.

# SESSION 1-4

## God's Rescue Plan for Humankind

*The Central Christian belief is that Christ's death has somehow put us right with God and given us a fresh start.*

*–C.S. Lewis,* Mere Christianity, *Book 2, Chapter 4*

## Questions to Explore

1. What did Jesus come to earth to do?

2. What did Jesus accomplish through His life, death, resurrection, and ascension?

3. How can we understand the concept of atonement?

4. How do I know if my sins have been forgiven through Jesus Christ's redemptive work on the cross?

## Bible Study

The apostle Paul in the book of Romans sheds light on God's rescue plan for humankind through Jesus Christ. Read the following verses from the book of Romans that have been described as "the Roman Road" and answer the questions that follow.

Romans 3:10–12, 23:

1.  Are human beings good enough on their own to be in relationship with God? Why or why not?

2.  Who is in need of salvation?

3.  How are we sinners both by nature and by choice?

Romans 6:23:

1.  What are the consequences of sin?

2.  Knowing this, how serious should we take the sin in our lives and in the lives of others?

3.    What is the gift that is offered to sinners?

4.    What does it cost us to get the gift of salvation?

Romans 5:8:

1.    How do we know that God loves us?

2.    How does the fact that He loves us, even though we have rebelled and sinned against Him, make you feel?

3.    How would you describe God's rescue plan for human beings?

4.    What did Jesus Christ do to make salvation possible for human beings?

Romans 10:9-10, 13:

1.  What does it mean to confess with one's mouth that Jesus is Lord?

2.  What does it mean to believe in one's heart that Jesus is Lord?

3.  How can we call upon the Lord?

4.  What is the means for a person to be saved?

Romans 5:1; 8:1, 38-39:

1.  What are the benefits of salvation for the person who surrenders and puts his or her trust in Jesus Christ?

2.   How do these benefits manifest themselves in a follower of Jesus' life?

3.   How is God's love made known through His rescue plan for humankind?

## Study of *Mere Christianity*

Read book 2, chapter 4, "The Perfect Penitent," in *Mere Christianity*. Answer the following questions in response to your reading:

1.   Assuming that Jesus was and is God in human form, what was His purpose for landing on this enemy-occupied world? What did Jesus come to do on earth?

2.   Who is "the perfect penitent"? In this chapter Lewis wrote, "The central Christian belief is that Christ's death has somehow put us right with God and given us a fresh start." And, "We are told that Christ was killed for us, that His death has washed out our sins, and that by dying He disabled death itself. That is the formula. That is Christianity. That is what has to be believed." Is Lewis correct about this being the central belief of Christianity?

Why or why not? How would you describe the central
belief of Christianity in your own words?

3.    What is "the hole" that human beings have gotten
      themselves into and are unable to get out of on their
      own?

4.    Observing the world around us, what indicators can
      we see that would back up Lewis's idea that all human
      beings are sinful and have rebelled against God?

5.    The atonement, "at-one-ment," is the idea that Jesus has
      made it possible for our sins to be forgiven as a result of
      His death on the cross and resurrection, which conquered
      sin, Satan, and evil. Name and explain some ways people
      have used to explain the idea of the atonement.

6.    How would you explain the atonement to someone?

7.  How does Lewis counter the people who discount Jesus' sufferings and death by saying, "if Jesus was God as well as man . . . 'it must have been so easy for Him'"?

8.  Have you accepted what Jesus Christ has done on your behalf through His death and resurrection and asked Him to be your Lord and Savior? Why or why not?

## Action Steps

1.  If you haven't surrendered to Jesus, would you like to do so now? If the answer is yes, you can do so by praying from the heart the following prayer. You may want to pray it out loud along with your study partners. "Dear God, I confess that I am a sinner. I know that my sin deserves the punishment of death. I believe that Jesus Christ is the Son of God and that He died on the cross for my sins, was buried, and rose again from the dead. I want to turn from my sins and trust Jesus Christ alone as my Savior. Thank You for the forgiveness of my sins and the gift of eternal life that I can now receive through faith in Jesus' name. Amen." By confessing with your mouth and believing in your heart that Jesus is Lord, you have now entered into a new life and relationship with Jesus Christ. You are now a disciple of Jesus and are on a lifelong journey of love for and obedience to your Lord and Savior. It is important for you to share what you have done with a friend, such

as the person walking with you through this study. Write down right now at least one action step following your discussion.

2.     Commit to praying daily and asking God to show you His truth and wisdom.

## Bible Memory Verse

"If you confess with your mouth that Jesus is Lord and believe in your heart that God raised him from the dead, you will be saved" (Romans 10:9).

## Concluding Observations on "the Roman Road" and Book 2, Chapter 4 of *Mere Christianity*

The apostle Paul in the book of Romans clarifies the reality of the human condition. We are all sinners and have been separated from God, our Creator. The consequence of our sin is death, both physical and spiritual. For human beings to be saved from death and for this relationship with God to be restored, we must admit that we are sinners who have turned away from God through our sinful words, thoughts, and actions. We must repent of our sins, die to ourselves, and by grace, through faith, place our trust in Jesus Christ for the forgiveness of our sins. When we confess with our mouths and believe in our hearts that Jesus is Lord, we are given the gift of eternal life with God.

The good news is that while we were sinners, God in His love and mercy, sent His Son, Jesus Christ, to be born of a virgin, to take on human flesh, live a perfect life, and then die for our sins, taking upon Himself the consequences of our sin. He atoned for our sin, took our place on the cross as our substitute. He then conquered sin, death, and the devil through His resurrection from the dead.

The Bible gives several analogies to help us understand this amazing work of grace on our behalf. He redeemed us, ransomed us, and saved us. The doctrine of the atonement is one to continually reflect upon in a spirit of gratitude and praise to God.

# SESSION 1-5

## Finding New Life in Christ

*A Christian is not a man who never goes wrong, but a man who is enabled to repent and pick himself up and begin over again after each stumble—because the Christ-life is inside him, repairing him all the time, enabling him to repeat (in some degree) the kind of voluntary death which Christ Himself carried out.*

–*C.S. Lewis*, Mere Christianity, *Book 2, Chapter 5*

## Questions to Explore

1.  Once a person surrenders to Christ as Lord, how does that person become more like Jesus?

2.  What should a Christian do?

3.  What is the fate of those who never had the opportunity to learn of Jesus?

4.  Why isn't God invading the world and conquering the devil with overwhelming force?

## Bible Study

Read Acts 2:37-47. Background: Jesus had told His disciples to wait in Jerusalem until He sent the Holy Spirit to empower them to proclaim the good news and make disciples locally and globally. At the Jewish celebration of Pentecost, the Holy Spirit fell upon the disciples; Peter stood up in the midst of the crowd and told them how God had fulfilled His promises and plan for the salvation of many as foretold through the Hebrew Scriptures: Through signs and wonders, Jesus of Nazareth had attested to His power as God's Son. Crucified by the people in Jerusalem, He had died and after three days risen from the dead. Peter told how he and the other disciples had witnessed the resurrected Christ and worshiped Him as Lord and God. Upon hearing this news, many in the crowd responded by asking how they could be saved. This passage follows Peter's evangelistic sermon.

Answer the following questions based on your reading of Acts 2:37-47:

1.  What did those who were "cut to the heart" by Peter's message ask?

2.  What was Peter's answer to their question?

3.  What is repentance?

4.    What is baptism?

5.    Read Romans 6:3–5. What does baptism symbolize?

6.    To what were the new disciples of Jesus devoted, leading to their growth?

7.    Where can we read and study "the apostles' teaching"? Why is it important for a follower of Jesus to seriously study this teaching?

8.    Why is it important to "fellowship" and spend time with other followers of Christ?

9.    Why is it important to "break bread" and celebrate the Lord's Supper, also known as Communion or the Eucharist, as a follower of Jesus?

10. Why is it important to pray to God as a regular part of the Christian life?

11. What else did the disciples of Jesus do as part of their obedience to Jesus?

12. How are their attitudes described by Luke, the author of the Acts of the Apostles?

13. What was the by-product of the lives of the early Christians?

## Study of *Mere Christianity*

Read book 2, chapter 5, "The Practical Conclusion," in *Mere Christianity*. Answer the following questions in response to your reading:

1. How was Jesus able to undergo the perfect surrender and humiliation and in so doing provide the means of salvation to all who put their trust in Him?

2. What is the next step for the new Christian believer?

3. How do we begin to live like Jesus Christ?

4. How does the "Christ life" grow in us and spread to others?

5. What does it mean to believe something based on the authority of Jesus? Why is it important for the follower of Jesus to trust Jesus' authority and obey His commands?

6. What is the role of baptism, faith, and the Lord's Supper in the Christian's life? Why are they important to a Christian's spiritual life? C.S. Lewis defines a Christian

as "not a man who never goes wrong, but a man who is enabled to repent and pick himself up and begin over again after each stumble—because the Christ-life is inside him, repairing him, all the time, enabling him to repeat (in some degree) the kind of voluntary death which Christ Himself carried out." Do you agree with this definition? Why or why not?

7.   How does a Christian become good?

8.   Why does God use physical matter such as bread, wine, and water to help us grow spiritually?

9.   What is the only means by which a person can be saved, forgiven, and receive eternal life? What implications does this have for the Christian in the way one shares one's faith?

10.   What happens to those who have never had the opportunity to hear of Christ? What is C.S. Lewis's response to this question?

11.   Why isn't God invading the world and conquering the devil with overwhelming force today?

12.   Lewis states that Jesus will come again at the end of the world; when He does, "it will be God without disguise; something so overwhelming that it will strike either irresistible love or irresistible horror into every creature. It will be too late then to choose your side." What is your response to this description of the return of Christ?

## Action Steps

1. At the end of this chapter, Lewis says, "Now, to-day, this moment, is our chance to choose the right side. God is holding back to give us that chance. It will not last for ever. We must take it or leave it." What is your response to this challenge from Lewis that we must make the choice to surrender to God now or possibly miss the opportunity?

2. Write down right now at least one action step in response to this session. For example, if you've decided to surrender your life to Jesus, you may decide to pursue baptism at a local church or partake in the Lord's Supper regularly at a local church.

3. Set aside five minutes daily, preferably first thing in the morning, to read a passage of Scripture and pray. Ask the Lord to guide you in establishing a daily devotional time.

4. Commit to praying daily and asking God to show you His truth and wisdom.

## Bible Memory Verse

"And they devoted themselves to the apostles' teaching and the fellowship, to the breaking of bread and the prayers" (Acts 2:42).

## Concluding Observations on Acts 2:37–47 and Book 2, Chapter 5 of *Mere Christianity*

When someone receives by grace, through faith in Jesus Christ, the gift of eternal life and the forgiveness of sins, that person is a new creation. The Christian is called to live like Jesus and to look like Him in the way he or she talks and lives. Why don't new Christians suddenly live perfect lives? Although we have been declared righteous through the work of Christ on our behalf, when we are born again we are like newborns who must grow up and gradually mature. So the Christian life is one in which we begin to look more and more like Jesus as we allow the "Christ-life" and the Holy Spirit to work within us daily. God has given us some helpful disciplines that are means of grace for us to grow. These include worshiping regularly with other Christians, being baptized, participating regularly in the Lord's Supper, reading Scripture, prayer, and service to one another.

Some people ask questions such as, what about the people who have never heard the gospel—what does God do with them? Lewis advises us to act on what we know. We know that no one comes into a relationship of reconciliation with God without believing in Jesus Christ. So let's focus on sharing the good news and leave the answers to questions that are unknown for God to handle and reveal in His time.

Some ask why God is taking His time in redeeming the world. Lewis hints that it may be a result of God's patience and grace to give more people the opportunity to repent and believe the good news. He also warns that it would not be wise to put off a decision about God, as we never know when Jesus will return to judge the living and the dead.

# SESSION 1-6

## Finding Your Place in the Church

*When you have reached your own room, be kind to those who have chosen different doors and to those who are still in the hall. If they are wrong they need your prayers all the more; and if they are your enemies, then you are under orders to pray for them. That is one of the rules common to the whole house.*

*—C.S. Lewis, Mere Christianity, Preface*

### Questions to Explore

1. What is the original meaning of the name Christians?

2. What is "mere" Christianity?

3. Why is it important to find a local church community with which to get involved?

4. How are we to treat other Christians in other denominations?

## Bible Study

Read Hebrews 10:19-25. Answer the following questions based on your reading:

1.  In this passage, whom is the writer of Hebrews addressing? Why is this important to know?

2.  Who is able to enter into the presence of God? Does this include you? Why or why not?

3.  What did Jesus do that enables us to enter into the house of God? Describe in detail His work on our behalf.

4.  What is expected from us in order to enter the house of God?

5.  What enables us to remain firm in our faith in Christ without wavering? Why is it important to remind ourselves of this as we live out our faith over the years?

6.    What are we commanded as Christians to do regularly with one another?

7.    Have you been stirred up, or spurred, to love and good deeds by other followers of Jesus? If so, describe. If not, why do you think that is?

8.    Why is it important for Christians to meet together regularly? What benefits do we gain from meeting together?

9.    What dangers are there for the Christian who fails to meet regularly with other Christians for prayer, fellowship, worship, and service?

10. The writer of Hebrews addresses some who call themselves "Christian" and have stopped meeting together. How would you encourage people like this today to get involved in a local church to pray, worship, and fellowship with other Christians?

11. What and when is "the Day drawing near"? What are Christians to be doing to prepare for this "Day"?

12. Have you been meeting regularly with other Christians? If not, what steps can you take to change this pattern? If yes, describe how meeting together with other followers of Jesus has affected your life.

## Study of *Mere Christianity*

Read the preface to *Mere Christianity*. Answer the following questions based on your reading:

1. What does Lewis present as the goal or purpose of his radio broadcasts and eventually the book *Mere Christianity*?

2. How does Lewis define "mere" Christianity?

3. Why does Lewis avoid speaking about disputed matters of doctrine among Christians in this book? Are there times when it is all right to discuss disputed matters of doctrines with other Christians? If so, when and how should we do that?

4. Lewis was an English professor who believed that it was important to be clear about the meaning of a word, especially when its meaning was distorted, changed, or adapted to fit new situations. He gives the example of the word *gentleman*. He then moves to the word *Christian*, which has come to mean many different things depending on who uses it. How does Lewis define the word *Christian?*

5. Why is it important to Lewis that the definition of *Christian* be tied to its original meaning as found in the New Testament?

6.    What definitions of the word *Christian* have you encountered that do not align with the definition as found in the New Testament and used by Lewis?

7.    What dangers should we avoid in trying to assess whether a person is a Christian?

8.    Lewis describes "mere" Christianity as the hallway of the church (all those who have accepted the apostles' teaching—the beliefs that have been common to all Christians at all times in human history since Christ walked the earth). Why doesn't Lewis give any advice about denominations (the rooms that extend off the hallway)?

9.    Why does Lewis encourage Christians not to remain in the "hallway," where they would have no commitment to a local church—one of the rooms off the hallway?

10. What recommendations does Lewis give for finding the kind of church that will help you as a Christian to grow and be fruitful?

11. Once you've chosen a local church or denomination, what should your attitude and actions be toward those in other congregations and denominations?

12. Have you experienced the unity that comes from worshiping with Christians from different denominations? If so, describe the experience and the relationships.

## Action Steps

1. Have you found a congregation of Christians with whom you can pray, worship, and serve? If not, what steps can you take this week to begin looking for a local church that upholds the authority of the Bible and the truth of the apostles' teaching? If yes, in what new ways might the Lord be leading you to get further involved in your local church?

2.    Take time to pray for two or three other Christians whom you know personally. Consider how you might encourage them this week with a call, a note, or a meal together.

3.    Commit to praying daily and asking God to show you His truth and wisdom.

**Bible Memory Verse**

"And let us consider how to stir up one another to love and good works, not neglecting to meet together, as is the habit of some, but encouraging one another, and all the more as you see the Day drawing near" (Hebrews 10:24-25).

**Concluding Observations on Hebrews 10:19-25 and the Preface of *Mere Christianity***

The original, New Testament meaning of the word *Christian* refers to a person who is a disciple of Jesus Christ and accepts the doctrines and teaching of the apostles as found in the Holy Scriptures. It is important to focus on the unity that followers of Jesus from different denominations have through their mutual relationship with God the Father through Jesus the Son. The writer of the book of Hebrews assures true followers of Jesus that their sins have been washed clean by the blood of Christ through His redemptive death and resurrection. Their hearts are clean in the sight of God. The great Priest, Jesus, makes it possible for us to enter with confidence into the presence of God. Therefore we must hold on to our faith and live with hope. In response to what Christ has done for us, we should meet regularly with other Christians in worship and to spur one another toward love and good deeds. C.S. Lewis speaks of "mere" Christianity as those essential teachings of the apostles that unite all true Christians (as defined in the New Testament) regardless of denomination. Lewis wisely counsels Christians to find a local church to belong to and to get involved in, gaining and giving the benefits of being among the community of saints. He recommends finding a church that teaches biblical truth and reflects the holiness of God in actions and words. When we differ in secondary teachings or practices from other Christians, we should pray for them and love them as brothers and sisters in the family of God.

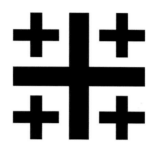

# PART 2: CHRISTIAN BEHAVIOR

A Study of *Mere Christianity*:
"Christian Behaviour"

# SESSION 2-1

## Morality and the Greatest Commandment

*Moral rules are directions for running the human machine.*

*Morality, then, seems to be concerned with three things. Firstly, with fair play and harmony between individuals. Secondly, with what might be called tidying up or harmonising the things inside each individual. Thirdly, with the general purpose of human life as a whole: what man was made for: what course the whole fleet ought to be on: what tune the conductor of the band wants it to play.*

*–C.S. Lewis,* Mere Christianity, **Book 3, Chapter 1**

## Questions to Explore:

1.  What is morality?

2.  Why are moral rules and obedience to them important?

3.  What are the three relationships that are tied to our moral behavior?

4.  What is the basis for Christian morality?

5. How does Christian morality differ from other forms of morality?

6. Why is the human person so valuable?

**Preparation for session:** Read the following Bible study passage and chapter in *Mere Christianity* on your own. Write answers to the accompanying questions that will be used in your upcoming discipleship meeting to help guide your discussion of the themes, truths, and ideas being presented. To love and serve those in your study, come prepared to actively discuss what you've discovered, listen to the insights of others, and pray for one another. Ask the Holy Spirit to guide and teach you as you seek to know and live out the truth. Remember that you are living in "enemy-occupied territory," so be aware of potential distractions or temptations that might hinder your spiritual growth. Be faithful, available, and teachable, so you can become a more effective disciple of Jesus Christ. Follow this same approach for each subsequent session.

## Bible Study

Read Mark 12:28-34. Answer the following questions based on your biblical reading:

1. What is Jesus' reply to the question, "Which commandment is the most important of all?" (v. 28)?

2. Jesus quotes the "Shema" from Deuteronomy 6:4-5, the Scripture passage that is put on the doorposts of Jewish

homes. It commands the people of Israel to love the Lord their God with all of one's heart, soul, and strength. Jesus adds a fourth part to loving God: with all of one's mind. Why is it important to love God with all four of these aspects of one's personhood? How is each aspect significant, playing a role in the way we demonstrate our love for God? Give some examples of loving God with each aspect.

3.    Why do you think Jesus answers the scribe's question with two commandments rather than one?

4.    How are the two commandments to love God and to love neighbor intertwined?

5.    What three categories of people are we to love according to these two commandments?

DISCIPLESHIP with C.S. LEWIS

6.    Do you love yourself? How do you show this?

7.    How is loving yourself connected to loving others? How is loving others connected to loving yourself?

8.    How do you love others?

9.    The scribe is praised by Jesus for understanding that loving God and his neighbor as himself is more important than burnt offerings and sacrifices. Why is obeying these two commandments so important?

10.    Matthew 22:34-40 is a parallel statement of the Great Commandment. Verse 40 says, "On these two commandments depend all the Law and the Prophets." What is this saying about the foundation of Christian morality?

**Study of *Mere Christianity***

Read book 3, chapter 1, "The Three Parts of Morality," in *Mere Christianity*. Answer the following questions in response to your reading:

1.    According to Lewis, what are morals?

2.    Why are moral directions needed for the "human machine"?

3.    Why does Lewis insist that morals are not ideals subject to our opinion or taste but rather moral rules or absolutes that are applicable to all?

4.    Why does Lewis argue that moral rules and obedience to them are essential to healthy human relationships?

5.	What is the result of moral failure to ourselves and those around us?

6.	What are the three parts of morality described by Lewis?

7.	Describe how Lewis uses the analogy of a fleet of ships sailing on a common course to help us understand the three parts of morality. Similarly describe his use of a musical band of instruments playing the same tune.

8.	The first part of morality deals with the harmonious relationship among individuals. What is the Christian moral ideal for human relationships?

9.	The second part of morality addresses the inner life, the thoughts and attitudes of the heart and mind. What is the Christian moral ideal for the things inside each individual?

10. The third part takes into account what our Creator has designed us to be and do. What is the Christian moral ideal for our relationship with our Creator?

11. Lewis states that "different beliefs about the universe lead to different behaviour . . . religion involves a series of statements about facts, which must be either true or false. If they are true, one set of conclusions will follow about the right sailing of the human fleet: if they are false, quite a different set." If this is true, why are a person's religious beliefs or lack thereof still important when it comes to moral behavior?

12. How does Christian morality value each human being? Why?

13. Why is a person of more value than a state, nation, or civilization?

14. Read again the last, summarizing paragraph in this Lewis chapter. Do you agree with him? Why or why not? What can you observe in the world around you that would prove Lewis's assessment to be fair as regards people's views about morality?

15. Contrast Christian morality and the predominant views of morality in our culture today. Relying on Lewis's assessment, analyze the "why" behind the differences.

## Action Steps

1. Take time to reflect on your love relationship with God. In what areas would you like to grow in your love for God?

2. Take time to reflect on your relationships with others. Is there anyone you have trouble loving? Pray and ask God for help and for practical ways to love this person.

3.  How well do you love yourself? Ask the Lord to help you love yourself and to see yourself from His perspective—as a child of God.

4.  Commit to praying daily and asking God to show you His truth and wisdom.

## Bible Memory Verses

"'Which commandment is the most important of all?' Jesus answered, 'The most important is, "Hear, O Israel: The Lord our God, the Lord is one. And you shall love the Lord your God with all your heart and with all your soul and with all your mind and with all your strength." The second is this: "You shall love your neighbor as yourself." There is no other commandment greater than these'" (Mark 12:28-31).

## Concluding Observations on Mark 12:28-34 and Book 3, Chapter 1 of *Mere Christianity*

"Christian Behaviour" begins with a discussion of morality—definitions and foundational principles. C.S. Lewis states that morality deals with our relationships with one another, our relationship with our Creator, and our inner thoughts and motivations. Different worldviews approach morality differently according to their understanding of God and whether moral laws are considered to be absolute or relative. Christians believe that moral laws are rules made by God for our well-being and the health of human relationships. Moral laws are not subject to our own personal tastes or choices. They are not relative but rather absolute and universal to all people at all times. God has given us very clear moral rules that, if obeyed, will bring happiness and healthy relationships. On the flip side, when moral rules are disobeyed, human relationships, society, and our relationship with God become dysfunctional and broken. Jesus summarized the Christian view of morality and healthy relationships when He stated that the two greatest commandments are to love God and to love our neighbor as we love ourselves. True love for someone else stems from our innermost being and is reflected in our actions. Thus love and morality affects the whole person.

# SESSION 2-2

## Wisdom and the Cardinal Virtues

*God is no fonder of intellectual slackers than of any other slackers. If you are thinking of becoming a Christian, I warn you, you are embarking on something which is going to take the whole of you, brains and all.*

*—C.S. Lewis,* Mere Christianity, *Book 3, Chapter 2*

## Questions to Explore

1.  Where can we get wisdom?

2.  Why are the "cardinal" virtues of such great moral importance for the Christian?

3.  What are prudence, temperance, justice, and fortitude?

4.  Why is the development of the Christian mind as important as the development of the heart?

## Bible Study

Read Proverbs 1:1-7; 2:1-22. Answer the following questions based on your scriptural reading:

1.   What is "the fear of the LORD"? Why is it so important to a virtuous life?

2.   Why is it so important to seek wisdom and wise instruction?

3.   The writer of Proverbs suggests we pursue wisdom by or through what ways?

4.   How do we learn to become just people who pursue justice?

5.   How do we learn to use discernment in making decisions?

6.   What are the results of a virtuous, wise life in which God's instruction is obeyed?

7.   What are the curses for those who ignore God's wisdom and behave in ways contrary to God's law and justice?

8.   In what ways have you learned from and been blessed by God's wisdom?

9.   In what ways would you like to grow in your understanding of God's wisdom?

## Study of *Mere Christianity*

Read book 3, chapter 2, "The 'Cardinal Virtues,'" in *Mere Christianity*. Answer the following questions in response to your reading:

1.   What are the four cardinal virtues?

2. Why do you think Classical thinkers saw these four virtues as the "pivotal" virtues in a person's life?

3. What is prudence?

4. Lewis wrote, "God is no fonder of intellectual slackers than of any other slackers. If you are thinking of becoming a Christian, I warn you, you are embarking on something which is going to take the whole of you, brains and all." How can we become intellectually lazy?

5. Why does God care so much about our minds and intellect?

6. What is the true meaning of temperance?

7.   Why is temperance more a motivation of the heart than something demonstrated by external actions?

8.   In what ways have you displayed temperance in your life?

9.   What is justice?

10.   What is the difference between doing a just action and being a just person?

11.   What is fortitude?

12.   How have you displayed justice or fortitude in your life?

13. How can right actions done for the wrong reason or motivation not be considered a virtue?

14. What do the presence of virtues or lack thereof in a person say about that person's relationship with Jesus and ability to experience the joy that God desires for people?

## Action Steps

1. Read one chapter of the book of Proverbs daily for a month. (There are thirty-one chapters.) Ask God to help you grow in wisdom, understanding, and virtue.

2. Write down right now at least one action step to complete following your discussion.

3. Write down right now any questions you would like to discuss at a later time.

4. Commit to praying daily and asking God to show you His truth and wisdom.

## Bible Memory Verse

"The fear of the LORD is the beginning of knowledge; fools despise wisdom and instruction" (Proverbs 1:7).

## Concluding Observations on Proverbs 1:1-7; 2:1-22 and Book 3, Chapter 2 of *Mere Christianity*

For Christians to behave in obedience to God's moral laws, they must first fear the Lord—revere Him and be in awe of His power, majesty, and wisdom, acknowledging that God knows better than we do. When we fear the Lord and submit to His commands, we are able to gain knowledge and apply that knowledge wisely. The book of Proverbs is full of wisdom for the person who desires to please God through his or her behavior. By reading, understanding, and applying the practical wisdom found in the book of Proverbs and throughout the Scriptures, we can make wise, just, and loving decisions. This will enable us to behave in ways that care for and serve those in need and promote peaceful living among human beings. In the early church, Christian behavior was divided into seven "virtues." The first four are the cardinal or pivotal virtues: prudence, temperance, justice, and fortitude. The next three are called the theological virtues: faith, hope, and charity (love). If we are to live virtuous lives, we must seek to give God control of our hearts and minds. God expects us to use our brains and not to be intellectually lazy. We must learn how to behave and think in a virtuous fashion as it is often contrary to our sinful nature.

Note that God is not concerned only about our external actions; He desires that our hearts have pure and righteous motivations. Thus God calls the Christian to be in training for heaven while here on earth; that is, to seek to live out the virtues of prudence, temperance, justice, and fortitude, being strongly committed to doing what is right.

# SESSION 2-3

## Social Morality and the Golden Rule

*I do not believe one can settle how much we ought to give. I am afraid the only safe rule is to give more than we can spare.*

—C.S. Lewis, *Mere Christianity, Book 3, Chapter 3*

## Questions to Explore

1. Did Jesus preach a new kind of morality?

2. What is the Golden Rule?

3. How should a follower of Christ love his or her neighbor?

4. How should the follower of Jesus practice the virtue of charity - giving to the poor?

5. What is the starting point for the Christian for living a moral life?

## Bible Study

Read Matthew 7:12 and Luke 10:25-37. Answer the following questions based on your scriptural reading:

1.  Restate the Golden Rule in your own words.

2.  Give an example of the Golden Rule being put into practice.

3.  Jesus commends the lawyer in Luke 10 for seeing the importance of loving God and neighbor. The lawyer, however, has a desire "to justify" himself, and he asks Jesus, "Who is my neighbor?" Why do you think the lawyer asked this question?

4.  Why does Jesus tell a parable to answer the lawyer's question?

5. What is the response of the two religious leaders, the priest and the Levite, when they pass by the man who has been beaten, stripped, and left for dead? Why do you think Jesus uses the religious leaders as the bad example in this story?

6. What is the response of the Samaritan (someone who was despised by the Jews for being half Jewish and half Syrian) to the man left for dead?

7. What does the Samaritan do to show his love for the injured man?

8. How generous is the Samaritan toward the injured Jewish man? Why do you think he is so generous?

9. From the parable of the Good Samaritan, what can we learn and apply to our daily lives?

## Study of *Mere Christianity*

Read book 3, chapter 3, "Social Morality," in *Mere Christianity*. Answer the following questions in response to your reading:

1. In what ways is Jesus' Golden Rule simple? Difficult?

2. How are we to apply the Golden Rule in our lives?

3. In what way should the Christian church give a lead or example in the application of the Golden Rule?

4. What should be the role of the clergy/pastors in the church?

5. What should be the role of the lay people in the church?

6.   What would be the traits of a "Christian society"?

7.   Lewis wrote, "Charity—giving to the poor—is an essential part of Christian morality." How much should Christians give of their time, talent, and treasure?

8.   Name some things that hinder us from being generous toward those in need. Toward the church. Toward other charitable causes.

9.   To what do you enjoy giving? Why?

10.  How could you give more of your time, talent, and treasure?

11.   Some approach Christianity in the hopes of finding support for their particular political view point. Why is this dangerous? How could it lead to negative behavior?

12.   What does Lewis mean by this statement: "A Christian society is not going to arrive until most of us really want it: and we are not going to want it until we become fully Christian"?

13.   Read the long sentence in the last paragraph of the chapter that begins: "I may repeat, 'Do as you would be done by' till I am black in the face . . ." Why is obedience to God the starting point in the progression of learning to love my neighbor as I love myself?

14.   How does our inner life affect our external behavior and the way in which we love those around us? How does our inner moral compass affect our social mores and choices?

## Action Steps

1.  Memorize the Golden Rule and post it where you'll see it daily. Then reflect and act upon it.

2.  Reflect upon your neighbors. Is there someone toward whom God may be calling you to be generous through a sharing of your time, talent, or treasure?

3.  Write down right now at least one action step to take this week.

4.  Commit to praying daily and asking God to show you His truth and wisdom.

## Bible Memory Verse

"So whatever you wish that others would do to you, do also to them, for this is the Law and the Prophets" (Matthew 7:12).

## Concluding Observations on Matthew 7:12 and Luke 10:25-37 and Book 3, Chapter 3 of *Mere Christianity*

Jesus gives the Christian a simple, practical, yet difficult approach to loving other people. He states in the Golden Rule (as popularly known), "Do unto others as you would have them do unto you." It is a positive, proactive statement that requires followers of Jesus to reach out in love to the neighbors around us through love and good deeds. He gives a wonderful picture of what this means through the parable of the Good Samaritan. In that story we see a Samaritan man care for a Jewish man (his enemy) who has been beaten by robbers. The Samaritan shares his time by going out of his way to care for him, his talent by giving first aid, and his treasure by giving the innkeeper money to care for the wounded man until the Samaritan can return. The church should reflect the Golden Rule in its actions. The church, and society for that matter, will never be fully healthy and loving until Christians are willing to surrender their time, talent, and treasure to God, love God, and love their neighbors (including their enemies) as they love themselves. If we love God, we will obey God and this will demonstrate itself through the loving thoughts, words, and actions of followers of Jesus.

**Note:** This study skips book 3, chapter 4, "Morality and Psychoanalysis." In this chapter Lewis compares the way Christianity seeks to change a person's behavior versus the approach of Freudian psychology. Lewis addresses some of the popular Freudian presuppositions that were popular in Lewis's day. He notes that Freud's philosophy is in direct contradiction to Christianity. Freud viewed belief in God as an unscientific coping mechanism that had no rational validity. Freud's practice of psychotherapy, however, is not necessarily contradictory to Christian morality. Both are seeking to "put the human machine right."

However, they go about it differently. Psychoanalysis seeks to change the way a person's subconscious perceives so that a person's reactions and behavior can be modified to behave normally rather than abnormally.

Lewis clarifies that Christian morality seeks to change people's behavior not by blindly and legalistically obeying a lot of rules, but rather through making consistent moral choices that enable you to act like and become a good person. As you make good moral choices over time, you behave more and more like a follower of Jesus. The inverse is true as well; if a person continues to make bad moral choices, he or she will become and behave more and more evil. In this chapter Lewis notes, "with all of your innumerable choices, all your life long you are slowly turning this central thing either into a heavenly creature or into a hellish creature: either into a creature that is in harmony with God, and with other creatures, and with itself, or else into one that is in a state of war and hatred with God, and with its fellow-creatures, and with itself."

Here Lewis also points out, "When a man is getting better he understands more and more clearly the evil that is still left in him. When a man is getting worse he understands his own badness less and less."

# SESSION 2-4

## Sexual Morality and the Virtue of Chastity

*Chastity is the most unpopular of the Christian virtues. There is no getting away from it: the old Christian rule is, "Either marriage, with complete faithfulness to your partner, or else total abstinence."*

*—C.S. Lewis, Mere Christianity, Book 3, Chapter 5*

### Questions to Explore

1.   What is the virtue of chastity?

2.   What is the Christian view of sexual intercourse?

3.   How does the Christian view of marriage and sexuality differ from that of the popular culture?

4.   What are the benefits of the Christian practice of chastity in which sex is reserved only to marriage between a man and woman?

5.   What are the harmful effects of sexual promiscuity and sexual immorality?

6.  How is our body a temple for the Holy Spirit? What are the implications of this?

## Bible Study

Read 1 Corinthians 6:12-20. Answer the following questions based on your reading:

1.  How is it that something can be lawful but not helpful to me? Give an example.

2.  What does Paul mean when he says, "I will not be enslaved/dominated by anything" (v. 12)?

3.  The Greek proverb "food is meant for the stomach and the stomach for food" (v. 13) is espousing, if I have a physical organ that has an appetite, it needs to be satisfied. Why does Paul indicate this is only partly true?

4.  Why is the Christian not to use the body in sexually immoral ways?

5. To whom does your body belong as a Christian? Why is this important? How does it shape the ways you use your body and handle your physical appetites for food, sex, and sleep?

6. How is this perspective different from the world's perspective today?

7. Why does Paul talk about the resurrection of the body in the midst of a passage on human sexuality?

8. Why is sexual intercourse outside of marriage sinful and harmful?

9. How is sexual intercourse more than just a physical act according to Paul?

10. Why do you think Paul uses the verb phrase *flee from* when facing sexual immorality? What happens if we don't take quick and strong flight from sexual temptation?

11. Why do sexual sins do so much damage to all parties involved?

12. How does knowing that the Holy Spirit resides within you as a Christian affect the way you view your body – the temple of the Holy Spirit?

13. How can we glorify God with our bodies?

## Study of *Mere Christianity*

Read book 3, chapter 5, "Sexual Morality," in *Mere Christianity*. Answer the following questions in response to your reading:

1. What is the rule of modesty or propriety?

2.   What practical advice does Lewis give to help young people and older people when societal standards of propriety change?

3.   How does Lewis define the Christian rule of chastity?

4.   In what ways does Lewis argue that our "sexual instinct" has gone wrong or has been distorted?

5.   How does our sexual appetite, like other appetites (for food or sleep), grow? How does our culture today encourage an excessive sexual appetite that results in many societal and personal sexual perversions and harmful consequences resulting from sexual activity outside of marriage?

6.   How does Christianity view the human body and the pleasure of sexual intercourse as compared to the other religions of the world?

7.  Why do Christians glorify marriage and create much of the world's greatest love poetry?

8.  What does the world's propaganda use to promote a warped view that all of our sexual desires are "healthy" and "natural"?

9.  Why would it be unhealthy and crazy to surrender to all of our desires without controlling them?

10. Lewis says, "The real conflict is not between Christianity and 'nature,' but between Christian principles and other principles in the control of 'nature.'" What is Lewis's point?

11. When we fail at attempting Christian chastity, what does God do for us if we seek His assistance?

12.  How is sexual repression different from suppressing a sexual desire for the purpose of living a sexually virtuous life?

13.  Why can those who attempt to live chaste lives sexually come to know more about their own sexuality than anyone else?

## Action Steps

1.  Lewis wrote, "A cold, self-righteous prig who goes regularly to church may be far nearer to hell than a prostitute. But, of course, it is better to be neither." How can you seek to live a sexually chaste life without being a self-righteous prig?

2.  In a prayerful mode, examine your sexual thoughts, desires, and actions. If any sin is revealed by the Holy Spirit, ask for God's forgiveness, pick yourself up again, and try living a life of Christian chastity again. Repeat as necessary.

3.   How can you glorify God today with your body, "the temple of the Holy Spirit"?

4.   Commit to praying daily and asking God to show you His truth and wisdom.

**Bible Memory Verses**

"Or do you not know that your body is a temple of the Holy Spirit within you, whom you have from God? You are not your own, for you were bought with a price. So glorify God in your body" (1 Corinthians 6:19-20).

**Concluding Observations on 1 Corinthians 6:12-20 and Book 3, Chapter 5 of *Mere Christianity***

When it comes to sexual behavior and morality, Christians uphold the virtue of chastity. The word *chastity* is often confused with particular social or cultural rules on modesty. Modesty, however, may be defined differently in different cultures, whereas the rule of chastity is the same for all Christians at all times. Chastity, which promotes marriage between a man and a woman with complete spousal fidelity, or else total abstinence from sexual activity, is unpopular today. This seems "unnatural" or "impossible" to so many people. Yet God invented sex and it is not something to be ashamed of. Rather, it is to be celebrated within the context of marriage as a beautiful, holy, and pleasurable act.

Paul presents a solid rationale for chastity by stating that our bodies as Christians are holy: "temples" in which the Holy Spirit resides. So we are to use our bodies, which are sexual in nature, as God intended them to be used, for procreation and pleasure within the context of marriage. The marriage relationship is meant to be sacred, unique, and set apart by the fact that only in marriage do two people become one flesh. They are bound together physically, emotionally, and spiritually. Sexual promiscuity outside of marriage, while it may be pleasurable for a moment, ends up harming relationships and creating abnormal sexual appetites, which pervert, addict, and harm the body, mind, and spirit.

While it may be difficult to live a chaste life in this tempting world, it is possible by God's grace. And the person who seeks to honor God with his or her body, in attempting chastity, will know more about his or her sexuality than the one who indulges sexual appetite outside of marriage. Also, when a person fails and commits a sexually immoral sin, the Christian can ask for forgiveness, commit his or her body to the Lord again, and seek to be chaste in future relationships. All virtues are strengthened through training our souls to depend on God for the power to be obedient to His laws and ways. As Lewis says, "Virtue—even attempted virtue—brings light; indulgence brings fog."

**Note:** This study skips book 3, chapter 6, "Christian Marriage." In this chapter, Lewis makes the following points: The Christian idea of marriage is based on Christ's words that a husband and wife are to be regarded as "one flesh." This sexual union distinguishes their relationship from all others and thus sexual intercourse is to be enjoyed only within the lifelong commitment of the marriage union. Christianity affirms the permanence of marriage "till death us do part."

Lewis notes that while different Christian denominations may differ on whether or not divorce is allowed in certain situations, all would agree that it is a violent cutting up of the "one flesh." Thus it is not just a simple readjustment of partners or the dissolving of a business partnership, as some in modern culture would argue.

Christian marriage includes the practice of the virtue of justice, in that promises are to be kept for a lifetime. Marriage is not based solely on the idea of "being in love" but is also strengthened by commitment to the promises made.

# SESSION 2-5

## The Virtue of Charity–Part 1: Forgiveness and Loving Our Enemies

*I believe there is [a Christian virtue] even more unpopular [than chastity]. It is laid down in the Christian rule, "Thou shalt love thy neighbour as thyself." Because in Christian morals "thy neighbour" includes "thy enemy," and so we come up against this terrible duty of forgiving our enemies.*

–C.S. Lewis, *Mere Christianity*, Book 2, Chapter 7

## Questions to Explore

1.  What is the true meaning of forgiveness?

2.  How can I forgive my enemy?

3.  Do I have to like my enemies?

4.  Am I able to harm or kill my enemy in wartime?

5.  Will God forgive me if I don't forgive others?

**Bible Study**

Read Matthew 6:9-15 and Matthew 5:43-48. Answer the following questions based on your reading:

1. Jesus gives His disciples a model for prayer in Matthew 6:9-15 that many call the Lord's Prayer. Have you memorized this prayer? If not, it would be great to meditate upon it all this week and memorize it so that it can be an outline for your prayers.

2. "Our Father in heaven, hallowed by your name." What are we doing in prayer by beginning with these words?

3. Why is it important to praise and adore God?

4. The word *Father* is better translated here as "Daddy." What is Jesus telling us about God if we can call Him Daddy?

5.   "Your kingdom come, your will be done, on earth as it is in heaven." What is the meaning of these words? How can we pray this in our own words in our daily life?

6.   "Give us this day our daily bread." How would you pray this in your own words? Have you seen God's provision in your own life? If so, what has that looked like?

7.   "And forgive us our debts, as we also have forgiven our debtors." What are we asking God to do for us? What must we do first in order for God to forgive our sins?

8.   "And lead us not into temptation, but deliver us from the evil one." What is the meaning of this prayer? Who is the evil one?

9. After the Lord's Prayer, Jesus follows up with "For if you forgive others their trespasses, your heavenly Father will also forgive you, but if you do not forgive others their trespasses, neither will your Father forgive your trespasses." What does this mean?

10. Why do you think Matthew repeats this idea twice (once in the Lord's Prayer and again after its conclusion)?

11. How important do you think it is for the Christian to be a forgiving person? What are the consequences of not forgiving others?

12. How would you summarize Jesus' teaching in Matthew 5:43–48?

13. Who are your enemies? How can you love your enemies?

## Study of *Mere Christianity*

Read book 3, chapter 7, "Forgiveness," in *Mere Christianity*. Answer the following questions in response to your reading:

1.  Christianity teaches us that we are to forgive others, including our enemies. What is the consequence if we don't forgive others?

2.  Forgiving people can be hard to do, especially when they have wounded us. What are two things that Lewis suggests we can do to make it easier?

3.  How does loving myself affect the way I am called to love others, even my enemies?

4.  Do I have to think my enemies are nice? Why or why not?

5.  What does it mean to hate the sin but not the sinner?

6.  Are we as Christians able to hate cruelty, treachery, evil, and sin? Why or why not?

7.  Are we able to punish our enemies for wrongdoing and still forgive them?

8.  What is the difference between the words *kill* and *murder*?

9.  According to Lewis, is it possible to be a Christian and kill one's national enemy in wartime? Why or why not?

10. How does the Christian's approach to punishing, killing, or harming the enemy in wartime differ from other types or morality?

11. What is the eternal destiny of human beings? How does this affect the way we treat people on this earth?

12. According to Lewis, what does it mean to wish for someone else's good?

13. How can we love people who are unlovable?

## Action Steps

1. Ask God to show you if there is someone you need to forgive. If God shows you someone, ask for His help to forgive.

2. Do you have "enemies" in your life? How can you actively love them? Remember, loving people doesn't mean that you condone their behavior, necessarily think them nice, or find them lovable. But God's supernatural power through the Holy Spirit can help you find ways to love your enemies.

3.    Use the Lord's Prayer as an outline for your daily prayer time.

4.    Commit to praying daily and asking God to show you His truth and wisdom.

## Bible Memory Verses

## The Lord's Prayer (Adapted from Matthew 6:9-13)

*Our Father who art in heaven,*
*hallowed be thy Name.*
*Thy kingdom come.*
*Thy will be done,*
*on earth as it is in heaven.*
*Give us this day our daily bread.*
*And forgive us our trespasses,*
*as we forgive those who trespass against us.*
*And lead us not into temptation,*
*but deliver us from evil.*
*[For thine is the kingdom,*
*and the power, and the glory,*
*forever and ever.] Amen.*

## Concluding Observations on Matthew 6:9-15, Matthew 5:43-48, and Book 3, Chapter 7 of *Mere Christianity*

One of the most difficult and unpopular Christian virtues is the aspect of "charity" or "love" that calls us to love and forgive our enemies. In the Sermon on the Mount (Matthew 5-7), on several occasions Jesus repeats the command to forgive those who have sinned against us, saying that otherwise God will not forgive our sins. This is made especially clear in the Lord's Prayer, an essential part of Christian behavior and practice in which we are to pray, "Forgive us our debts, as we forgive our debtors" (traditional King James Version).

Christians are called to love their neighbors, which Jesus broadly defined in the parable of the Good Samaritan; the category includes our enemies. We are not called necessarily to like our enemies, to think of them as "nice." We are called to hate sin in people's lives (including our own), yet we are to love the sinner (including ourselves). We are called to love others with God's help even if they are unlovable. Lewis addresses the question of wartime, is it possible to kill our enemy and still love him? Lewis makes the case that it is possible to kill (not murder) one's enemy in battle. However, Christians, believing that all people are immortals who will become either heavenly or hellish creatures after death, must not enjoy punishing offenders or wartime killing or hate the enemy or combatant. We should always wish the other person's good and love that person as we would love ourselves.

# SESSION 2-6

## The Virtue of Humility and the Vice of Pride

*There is one vice of which no man in the world is free; which every one in the world loathes when he sees it in someone else; and of which hardly any people . . . ever imagine that they are guilty themselves . . .*

*The vice I am talking of is Pride or Self-Conceit: and the virtue opposite to it, in Christian morals, is called Humility.*

–C.S. Lewis, *Mere Christianity, Book 3, Chapter 8*

## Questions to Explore

1.  What is the vice of pride?

2.  What is the virtue of humility?

3.  What are the characteristics of pride?

4.  What are the characteristics of humility?

**Bible Study**

Read Philippians 2:1-11. Answer the following questions based on your reading:

1.  Paul is writing to the Christians in Philippi, a church he helped start. He asks that they "complete" his joy. How can they bring him joy?

2.  How is true Christian unity attained according to Paul?

3.  How does Paul define humility? What are the characteristics of humility?

4.  How can we regard others as more significant than ourselves? What does Paul mean by this?

5.  How can we look out for the interests of others more than for our own?

6.   How did Jesus exemplify humility? What did he do?

7.   Why did Jesus leave the majesty of heaven and humble Himself to go through all of the stages of human life starting as a fetus in the womb of Mary to a grown man walking on this dusty earth?

8.   How does Jesus' dying on the cross demonstrate his humility?

9.   What was the result of Jesus' acts of humility?

10.   How can we emulate Jesus and be a person of humility?

11.   To be a person of humility, to what must we die?

12.    Think of someone truly humble that you have known. How is it that you can identify them as humble?

## Study of *Mere Christianity*

Read book 3, chapter 8, "The Great Sin," in *Mere Christianity*. Answer the following questions in response to your reading:

1.    Why do we despise pride so much in other people?

2.    Is Lewis correct that the more pride we have, the more likely we are to dislike others who are proud?

3.    Why do Lewis and many Christian teachers view pride as the essential vice? How is pride at the center of morality or the root issue of morality?

4.    How is pride an anti-God state of mind? Give examples.

5.  How is pride competitive? Give examples.

6.  Why does Lewis argue that pride is the chief cause of misery in the world and the destroyer of relationships?

7.  How does pride keep one from truly knowing and worshiping God?

8.  How does pride creep into our religious life?

9.  What is the difference between being prideful and feeling pleasure when being praised by others?

10. Is it all right to be "proud" of one's son, daughter, or someone else?

11.   Why does God desire to see the virtue of humility in His children?

12.   What is the first step to acquiring humility?

13.   What does Lewis mean when he says, "If you think you are not conceited, it means you are very conceited indeed"?

14.   What does a truly humble person look like and act like?

## Action Steps

1.   Ask God to show you where pride is rearing its ugly head in your life. Ask for His forgiveness and grace to begin to display humility in your thoughts, words, and actions.

2. Take time to intentionally and authentically praise and highlight the excellent qualities and actions of others each day this week.

3. Consider how you might begin to put the interests of others before your own interests. Take intentional action to put this into practice.

4. Reflect on the humility of Jesus, His words and actions, and thank Him for giving up all in order to save you.

5. Commit to praying daily and asking God to show you His truth and wisdom.

## Bible Memory Verses

"Do nothing from rivalry or conceit, but in humility count others more significant than yourselves. Let each of you look not only to his own interests, but also to the interests of others. Have this mind among yourselves, which is yours in Christ Jesus" (Philippians 2:3-5).

## Concluding Observations on Philippians 2:1-11 and Book 3, Chapter 8 of *Mere Christianity*

Pride or self-conceit is the vice that Christian teachers view as "the Great Sin," as it seems to affect all areas of life and leads to every other vice or sin. The issue of pride is at the center of morality—the most crucial issue we must all address. And while we may be proud and unable to see it in ourselves, we identify it easily in others and despise them for it. Pride was the sin the devil introduced into the world and is the anti-God vice. The prideful person puts his or her own interests before God, desiring to be the one in control. Being competitive, pride is the chief cause of pain and suffering in the world as it brings about enmity among people and between people and God. The prideful person fails to see that God is superior in every way to us. Rather than worshiping God, the prideful person will find other things, including self, to worship, making it difficult for the prideful person to find and know God.

Jesus is the ultimate example of the virtue of humility, the opposite of pride. As the almighty, all-knowing, ever-present God, He humbled Himself and took on human flesh. He was conceived as a human fetus, born as a baby to Mary, and then lived among us. To further humiliate Himself, He willingly went to the cross and died for our sins. As a result of His obedience to God the Father and His humility, He is now exalted above all others. Jesus is our model, example, and leader in the way of humility. Many people misunderstand what pride and humility look like. There is a positive sense to the word *pride*, such as when we take pride in the successes of others, when we enjoy the praises of others without it "going to our head," and when we are able to delight in the gifts that God has given to us. Ultimately God wants us to be humble, so we can see ourselves as we truly are, get rid of the false self, and delight in who God has made us and enjoy our relationship with our awesome, loving Lord.

# SESSION 2-7

## The Virtue of Charity–Part 2

*Charity means "Love, in the Christian sense." But love, in the Christian sense, does not mean an emotion. It is a state not of the feelings but of the will; that state of the will which we have naturally about ourselves, and must learn to have about other people.*

–C.S. Lewis, *Mere Christianity, Book 3, Chapter 9*

### Questions to Explore

1. What are the theological virtues?

2. What is the meaning of the word *charity*? of the word *love*?

3. What does love look like, and how is it expressed?

4. What does God require of us in regard to love?

## Bible Study

Read 1 Corinthians 13:1-13. Answer the following questions based on your reading:

1.  What does Paul mean when he states that if I speak in other languages, have prophetic powers, have supernatural faith, and give everything away, yet have not love, I am nothing?

2.  Why is it important that our words, actions, and thoughts be based on love? What is the consequence if we do "good" things in an unloving manner?

3.  Can you share examples where you have seen "good" deeds done without love? What were the consequences?

4.  How many positive adjectives and adverbs does Paul use to describe love? What can you learn from these positive descriptions of love?

5. How many negative adjectives and adverbs does Paul use to describe what love is not? What can you learn from what love is not?

6. How do you measure up to this description of love in regard to your parents? Spouse? Children? Friends? In what areas do you need help to become a more loving person?

7. How is it that "love never ends"? What does Paul mean by this?

8. What does it mean that now we know only in part, but when perfection comes we will know in full?

9. What is so important about faith, hope, and love? Why is love the greatest of these three?

10. To what extent can we live up to this description of love? How can we do better at living a life of love?

## Study of *Mere Christianity*

Read book 3, chapter 9, "Charity," in *Mere Christianity*. Answer the following questions in response to your reading:

1. What are the three theological virtues? Why are these three virtues so important?

2. How has the definition of the word *charity* evolved over time?

3. What does love mean "in the Christian sense"?

4. Why do we naturally love ourselves and yet need to learn to love other people?

5.   How is Christian love for one's neighbor different from liking or having an affection for one's neighbor?

6.   How can liking someone lead to an unloving and unhealthy action or attitude toward someone else?

7.   What is the duty of learning charity? What is the rule that we are to follow according to Lewis?

8.   How does acting as if we loved our neighbor lead to the actual loving of our neighbor? How does the "cold" love of Christian charity lead to warm affection?

9.   How is the opposite true, that if we ill-treat people we will begin to hate them even more?

10. Why are the little decisions made daily of infinite importance? How do good and evil actions increase at compound interest?

11. What should we do if we don't have loving feelings toward others? Toward God?

12. How is loving God and loving neighbor an act of will? Why is this important for the Christian to understand?

13. Does God ever stop loving us? What are the implications of your answer to this question?

## Action Steps

1. Meditate upon 1 Corinthians 13 over the next week. Ask God to show you how you can grow in love toward Him and others.

2.  Be intentional about loving others, so you can learn to love others. Reach out especially in love toward someone you find it difficult to love.

3.  Ask a good friend how you might better love him or her through your words and actions.

4.  Pray daily 1 Corinthians 13:4-7, asking God to fill you with His love and these attributes of love.

5.  Commit to praying daily and asking God to show you His truth and wisdom.

## Bible Memory Verses

"Love is patient and kind; love does not envy or boast; it is not arrogant or rude. It does not insist on its own way; it is not irritable or resentful; it does not rejoice at wrongdoing, but rejoices with the truth. Love bears all things, believes all things, hopes all things, endures all things.

Love never ends" (1 Corinthians 13:4-8).

## Concluding Observations on 1 Corinthians 13:1-13 and Book 3, Chapter 9 of *Mere Christianity*

Love is the mark of the follower of Jesus Christ as he or she excels in love and good deeds toward others. Love in the Christian sense is not an emotion, a feeling, or a romantic idea, but rather an act of the will in which we choose to act lovingly toward others whether we feel like it or not. In fact, it is when we naturally don't feel an affection for someone yet love that person anyway that God's love is seen in us, as followers of Jesus. It is possible to do all kinds of good deeds and even perform supernatural acts, but if we don't do these things in a loving manner, they are worthless in their eternal value. God will not approve of these "good" deeds done without love. Love is also something we must learn to do, and the way we learn is through intentional, thoughtful acts of love toward others. The more we act with love toward others, the greater the likelihood that we will grow in affection toward them. In the same way, if we carelessly begin treating people badly, we can grow in enmity toward them, and God will not be pleased. We must be aware of the fact that all our actions lead toward good or evil and have a compounded effect in our lives and the lives of others.

The great assurance we have is that God's love for us never stops. He is always lovingly pursuing us. And once we know God's love, we are able to love, as Paul describes in 1 Corinthians 13, with patience, kindness, not exhibiting envy or boastfulness, arrogance or rudeness. We will not insist on our own way or be irritable or resentful. We won't rejoice in wrongdoing but will rejoice in the truth. We will bear all things, believe all things that are true, hope all things, and endure all things, as God's love for us never ends.

# SESSION 2-8

## The Virtue of Christian Hope

*If you read history you will find that the Christians who did most for the present world were just those who thought most of the next.*

—C.S. Lewis, *Mere Christianity, Book 3, Chapter 10*

## Questions to Explore

1. What is the virtue of hope?

2. How can we get the most out of life on earth?

3. What will heaven be like?

4. Why should we aim for heaven in order to be productive on earth?

## Bible Study

Read Colossians 3:1-17. Answer the following questions based on your reading:

1. Who has been raised with Christ?

2. What does it mean to set your mind on things above?

3. How will followers of Jesus be revealed with Him in glory?

4. How does seeking things above change the way we behave and live on earth?

5. What are we to put to death in our lives? What does this look like?

6. Why is the wrath of God coming upon the disobedient? Who were the disobedient, and who are now the disobedient?

7.   How do we strip off the old self and clothe ourselves with the new self?

8.   How are followers of Jesus Christ united? What types of people can become Christians?

9.   As disciples of Jesus, with what are we to clothe ourselves? What does this look like?

10.   As disciples of Jesus, how are we to deal with conflict among ourselves?

11.   How can we be obedient to the word of Christ and remind ourselves of His commands and teachings?

12. What does it mean to do everything in word and deed in the name of Jesus, giving thanks to God the Father?

13. What is the connection between living for Jesus now on this earth and focusing on heaven?

## Study of *Mere Christianity*

Read Book 3, Chapter 10, "Hope," in *Mere Christianity*. Answer the following questions in response to your reading:

1. What does Lewis mean when he states that those Christians who have done the most for this present world have been those who thought most of heaven?

2. How does aiming at heaven lead to greater good here on earth?

3. What do we get when we "aim at heaven"? What does this mean?

4. What do we get when we "aim at earth"? What does this mean?

5. Why do most Christians have a misunderstanding about heaven? What are the misconceptions?

6. How do our longings point to our desire for heaven?

7. Why do good things still leave us longing for more?

8.  What is the "Fool's Way" of dealing with our longings for more? Give examples, if possible, of your having seen this lived out.

9.  What is the "Way of the Disillusioned 'Sensible Man'"? Name ways you've seen this lived out.

10. What is the "Christian Way" of dealing with our longings?

11. What does Lewis mean when he says, "If I find in myself a desire which no experience in this world can satisfy, the most probable explanation is that I was made for another world"?

12. What do the symbols of music, crowns, and other symbols of heaven represent in the Bible? How do they help us grasp more about what heaven is like?

13. Describe the Christian hope of heaven. What does that hope look like? How does it inspire us on this earth to aim for heaven?

## Action Steps

1. How can you practice aiming for heaven each day this week? Write down right now some ideas to remind yourself that you are setting your mind on heavenly things.

2. Reflect on how a focus on our place with the Lord in glory in the future affects the way we live our lives now for Christ.

3. Describe how this hope of glory can help you get through difficult circumstances and comfort others during their times of loss or difficulty.

4.   How would you respond to someone who said, "You're too heavenly minded to be any earthly good"?

5.   Commit to praying daily and asking God to show you His truth and wisdom.

## Bible Memory Verses

"If then you have been raised with Christ, seek the things that are above, where Christ is, seated at the right hand of God. Set your minds on things that are above, not on things that are on earth. For you have died, and your life is hidden with Christ in God. When Christ who is your life appears, then you also will appear with him in glory" (Colossians 3:1-4).

## Concluding Observations on Colossians 3:1-17 and Book 3, Chapter 10 of *Mere Christianity*

Hope is the theological virtue that for the follower of Jesus is based on the firm conviction that this earthly life is not all there is. When we die, we will be raised up with Jesus and live forever with Him in heaven, the place of glory! This hope isn't pie-in-the-sky thinking but rather a truth that provides the follower of Jesus with the motivation and hope to live a joyful, loving life in service to God and others on this earth. Lewis notes that those followers of Jesus who have aimed for heaven have made the most impact for good here on earth. Those who are caught up focusing on earthly rewards, pleasures, and desires lose sight of all they could have by living with an eternal focus; what's more, they are not effective in helping others. When we are seeking to do everything in word and deed for the glory of Jesus' name while giving thanks to God our Father, we end up putting to death sinful thoughts, words, and deeds and live so as to reflect the goodness, love, and grace of God. Rather than looking for the next earthly thrill or prize or repressing our longings for meaning in life, the Christian is able to realize that earthly longings for "more" are really a longing for a heavenly home with Jesus. The desires we have will never be totally satisfied by worldly things. But when we die and are resurrected with Jesus Christ, we will finally realize the ultimate fulfillment of those longings. Heaven will not be a boring place, but rather a place of satisfying work, great joy, and a place filled with the loving presence of God. Thus the maxim that some people are too heavenly minded to be any earthly good is false. Rather, it is heavenly minded followers of Jesus who have the most potential to do good on this earth.

# SESSION 2-9

## The Virtue and Gift of Faith

*Christ offers something for nothing: He even offers everything for nothing. In a sense, the whole Christian life consists in accepting that very remarkable offer. But the difficulty is to reach the point of recognising that all we have done and can do is nothing.*

*–C.S. Lewis, Mere Christianity, Book 3, Chapter 12*

## Questions to Explore

1. What is faith?

2. What is the place of reason in faith? The place of the imagination and emotions?

3. What must a person do to be saved and forgiven of his or her sins?

4. What are the roles of faith and good works in the Christian life?

**Bible Study**

Read Ephesians 2:1-10. Answer the following questions based on your reading:

1.   What is the consequence of sins and trespasses in our lives? What does this mean?

2.   When we were dead in sin, who or what was influencing us? Describe these enemies of the soul.

3.   What was God's response when He saw that we were dead in sin? What does this tell you about the character of God?

4.   How can we be made alive, after being dead in sin?

5.   How is a follower of Christ saved from spiritual death?

6.   What is grace?

7.   What is faith?

8.   What part do we play in earning our salvation? Why is this important to know?

9.   What has God created us to do?

10.  When did God put a plan into motion for our lives? What kind of confidence does this give you?

## Study of *Mere Christianity*

Read book 3, chapter 11, "Faith," and chapter 12, "Faith," in *Mere Christianity*. Answer the following questions in response to your reading:

## Chapter 11—Faith

1.  What is the first level or sense of faith as explained by Lewis?

2.  What three faculties of the human person are used as a basis for faith?

3.  Why and how are these faculties at war with one another on occasion?

4.  Are the logical weight of evidence and the faculty of reason enough to sustain faith? Why or why not?

5.  How is faith a virtue?

6.  How do we handle mood swings in regard to our faith?

7. What spiritual disciplines are necessary to living a strong Christian life full of faith?

8. How can we keep from drifting away from our faith in Christ?

9. What do we learn from trying to live out the Christian virtues?

10. Why is Jesus the only complete realist who ever lived?

11. Is it possible on one's own to live a perfect life and "pass the exam" given in life?

12. What has been given to you by God? Why is that important to know?

13. What is your position in relation to God?

## Chapter 12–Faith (Part 2)

1. What does Lewis suggest that we do when we don't understand a Christian doctrine or teaching? How can you apply this in your life now?

2. What is the second sense or level of faith described by Lewis? Why does this level of faith arise "after a man has tried his level best to practise the Christian virtues, and found that he fails, and seen that even if he could he would only be giving back to God what was already God's own"?

3. What does it mean to discover our own bankruptcy?

4. What is the pivotal moment in the Christian life?

5.   What does it mean to lose confidence in our own ability to live a virtuous life and to leave it to God?

6.   How can we begin to look, act, and feel like Christ?

7.   What does it mean that Christ offers everything for nothing?

8.   When we fully trust Christ, what is our response to Him?

9.   Why is it essential for the Christian to obey Jesus? What does obedience indicate for the Christian?

10.  How do faith in Jesus and good actions and deeds relate to one another?

11. How do obedience and good deeds demonstrate authentic faith? Why do disobedience and evil deeds call into question a person's faith?

12. Why is Christianity ultimately more than just morality, duties, rules and guilt, and virtue? What is the something beyond that far surpasses it all?

## Action Steps

1. If you haven't surrendered to Jesus, would you like to do so now? If the answer is yes, then you can do so now by praying from the heart, the following prayer. You may want to pray it out loud along with your study partners.

   Dear God, I confess that I am a sinner. I know that my sin deserves the punishment of death. I believe that Jesus Christ is the Son of God and that He died on the cross for my sins, was buried, and rose again from the dead. I want to turn from my sins and trust Jesus Christ alone as my Savior. Thank You for the forgiveness of my sins and the gift of eternal life that I can now receive through faith in Jesus' name. Amen.

By confessing with your mouth and believing in your heart that Jesus is Lord, you have now entered into a new life and relationship with Jesus Christ. You are now a disciple of Jesus and are on a lifelong journey of love and obedience to your Lord and Savior. It is important for you to share what you have done with a friend, such as the person going through this study with you.

2.   Describe how you have experienced God's love for you.

3.   Describe how you have battled against the world, the flesh and the devil and how the Holy Spirit has helped you overcome temptation.

4.   Describe how your obedience to Christ's commands reflects your faith in Him.

5.   Commit to praying daily and asking God to show you His truth and wisdom.

## Bible Memory Verses

"For by grace you have been saved through faith. And this is not your own doing; it is the gift of God, not a result of works, so that no one may boast" (Ephesians 2:8-9).

## Concluding Observations on Ephesians 2:1-10 and Book 3, Chapters 11 and 12 of *Mere Christianity*

God loved us in that while we were still sinners—dead in sin—He loved us and sent Christ to lay down His life for us. It is by God's grace, through faith in Jesus, that we are saved, not by our works or good deeds. We have no reason to boast. God has offered us everything for nothing; it is undeserved, unmerited favor from God that allows us to believe in Jesus and put our trust in Him. This is what leads to our salvation from sin and death; we will one day be raised to new life with Jesus. Belief in Christ is reasonable but involves the mind and the heart (emotions, will, imagination). We must live out our faith by actively pursuing God and obeying His commands. In fact, our good deeds and loving actions are the indication that we truly have been saved. So while our salvation is not earned, our effort to obey Jesus is that which authenticates the fact of our salvation. We will be tempted to fall away from our relationship with God as the world, the devil, and our own sinful desires seek to lead us astray. This is why the spiritual disciplines of daily prayer, daily Bible reading and meditation, and regular (I suggest weekly) church attendance to worship God and fellowship with other believers are so important. They are means of grace by which we deepen our trust in Christ and begin to look more like Him. On our own strength, we are unable to live moral, virtuous lives. But by confessing our weakness and trusting in His strength and power, we can mature in our faith and turn our hearts' eyes on Jesus. When we are in love with Him and living for Him, we experience God's joy and are given a glimpse into eternity.

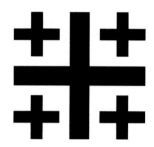

## PART 3: AN INTRODUCTION TO CHRISTIAN THEOLOGY AND DISCIPLESHIP

A Study of Book 4 of *Mere Christianity*:
"Beyond Personality: Or First Steps
in the Doctrine of the Trinity"

# SESSION 3-1

## Why Study Theology? & the Doctrine of Christ

*A great many of the ideas about God which are trotted out as novelties today are simply the ones which real Theologians tried centuries ago and rejected. To believe in the popular religion of modern England is retrogression—like believing the earth is flat.*

—C.S. Lewis, *Mere Christianity*, **Book 4, Chapter 1**

### Questions to Explore

1.   What is theology?

2.   Why is theology important for all Christians?

3.   What does it mean that Christ is the Son of God?

4.   What does it mean that we can become "sons of God"?

5.   What is the difference between "begotten" and "made"?

**Preparation for Session:** Read the following Bible study passage and chapter in *Mere Christianity* on your own. Write answers to the accompanying questions, which will be used in your upcoming discipleship meeting to help guide your discussion of the themes, truths, and ideas being presented. To love and serve those in your study, come prepared to actively discuss what you've discovered, listen to the insights of others, and pray for one another. Ask the Holy Spirit to guide and teach you as you seek not only to know truth, but also to live it out. Remember that you are living in "enemy-occupied territory," so be aware of potential distractions or temptations that might hinder your spiritual growth. Be faithful, available, and teachable so that you can become a more effective disciple of Jesus Christ. Follow this same approach for each subsequent session.

## Bible Study

Read John 1:1-18. Answer the following questions based on your reading:

1. Who is "the Word" or, in Greek, "the Logos" described in this passage?

2. What do we know about Jesus Christ's nature and character from this passage?

3. What role did Jesus have in the creation of the world?

4. What role did John the Baptist play in God's plan?

5. What does the description "true light" tell us about the nature of Jesus?

6. Why did many people in the world fail to recognize Jesus for who He was?

7. What gift is given to those who put their faith in Jesus?

8. What does it mean to be born of God?

9. What is the meaning of "the Word became flesh and dwelt among us" (v. 14)?

10.    In this passage what else does the apostle John tell us about Christ?

11.    How is Jesus different from Moses? Why is this important?

12.    How is God the Son distinct from God the Father?

## Study of *Mere Christianity*

Read book 4, chapter 1, "Making and Begetting," in *Mere Christianity*. Answer the following questions in response to your reading:

1.    What is theology? Lewis suggests anyone who thinks about God should study theology. Why?

2.    How is theology like a map? How is theology practical?

3. How does the study of theology keep people from repeating the errors of past thinkers?

4. If Jesus was merely a great moral teacher and Christianity merely a place to find good advice, why would Christianity be of no importance?

5. Three important teachings of the Christian faith are that (1) Christ is the Son of God; (2) those who put their confidence in Him can become "sons of God"; (3) Christ's death saved us from our sins. Why would it be important to study theology to know more about these doctrines of the faith?

6. The Bible teaches that Jesus is the Son of God. What does it mean that He was begotten not made?

7. How can we become "sons of God"?

8. What is the difference between biological life (*bios*) and spiritual life (*zoe*)?

9. How does the analogy of statues coming to life help us understand how God can make us into sons of God?

10. At the beginning of book 4, chapter 2, Lewis summarizes the previous chapter: "A man begets a child, but he only makes a statue. God begets Christ but He only makes men." What is Lewis trying to say about Christ's relationship to God the Father?

## Action Steps

1. Take time to thank God for sending His only begotten Son, Jesus, to live, die, and rise again. Meditate upon this great truth by reading John 1:1-18 daily for a week.

2.  Reflect upon how you would describe Jesus to a friend who had never heard of Him. Similarly reflect on how you would describe Him to a stranger.

3.  Commit to praying daily and asking God to show you His truth and wisdom.

## Bible Memory Verse

"And the Word became flesh and dwelt among us, and we have seen his glory, glory as of the only Son from the Father, full of grace and truth" (John 1:14).

## Concluding Observations on John 1:1-18 and Book 4, Chapter 1 in *Mere Christianity*

The study of theology is important for all Christians as it helps us better understand and know God. It doesn't have to be some dry academic exercise but can be very practical and helpful in everyday life. Even the basic truths of the faith, that Jesus is the Son of God, that He came to make us "sons of God," through His death and resurrection, are in need of theological explanations. Knowledge of the doctrine of Christ, the truth about who Jesus is and what He did, is essential for the Christian. The Gospel of John makes it clear that Jesus, "the Word," is fully God and that He, the Son of God, was active in the creation of the world along with God the Father. Jesus was begotten, not made. In other words,

He has existed eternally with the Father and yet is distinct from the Father. He was not created. Jesus Christ took on human flesh (the Incarnation) and lived among us on this earth. He came to reveal God's grace and truth and to provide a means of salvation from sin. When we put our trust in Christ and His atoning work on our behalf, we can become "sons of God" and are made spiritually alive—given eternal life to live forever in heaven with Christ.

# SESSION 3-2

## Understanding the Doctrine of the Trinity

*If Christianity was something we were making up, of course we could make it easier. But it is not. We cannot compete, in simplicity, with people who are inventing religions. How could we? We are dealing with Fact. Of course anyone can be simple if he has no facts to bother about.*

*—C.S. Lewis, Mere Christianity, Book 4, Chapter 2*

### Questions to Explore

1. What is the doctrine of the Trinity?

2. How does the fact that God is love reinforce the doctrine of the Trinity?

3. How do the three Persons of the Trinity relate to one another and yet remain one God?

4. Why is theology or the study of God both simple and complex?

**Bible Study**

The doctrine of the Trinity states that

1.  God eternally exists as three Persons, God the Father, God the Son, and God the Holy Spirit.

2.  Each Person of the Trinity is fully and equally God.

3.  There is one God.

This doctrine is progressively revealed through the Scriptures and is an essential tenet of Christian faith and teaching. Heresies or false teachings on this doctrine deny one or more of the three statements above. Orthodox or biblical teaching affirms all three statements as necessary and clearly representational of the true character and personhood of God as He is revealed to us in Scripture and through Jesus Christ.

Read the following Bible passages, which shed light on this essential doctrine of Christianity. After reading the passages, answer the questions.

Genesis 1:26; 3:22; 11:7; Isaiah 6:8:

1.  How is God revealed in each of these passages as being one God in three Persons?

2. Why is important to note that in the very first chapter of the Bible, God is clearly revealed through both individual and plural pronouns?

Isaiah 61:1; 63:10:

1. What do we learn about the Holy Spirit from these two passages?

Matthew 3:16-17:

1. What do we learn about God from the baptism of Jesus?

2. How are the three persons of the Trinity represented in this passage?

Matthew 28:19:

1. How does this passage highlight the centrality and essential nature of the Trinity in Christian faith and teaching?

2.   Why do you think Jesus commands that disciples
     be baptized (the initiation rite of the Christian and a
     sacrament of the church) in the name of the Father, the
     Son, and the Holy Spirit?

John 1:1-4:

1.   How is Jesus (the Word) distinct from God the Father?

2.   How was Jesus involved in the creation of the world?
     How was God the Father involved in the creation of the
     world?

1 Corinthians 12:4-6; Ephesians 4:4-6; 1 Peter 1:2; Jude 20-21

1.     What do we learn from these passages about each of the three Persons of the Trinity?

2.     What roles do each of the three Persons of the one God play?

## Study of *Mere Christianity*

Read book 4, chapter 2, "The Three-Personal God," and chapter 4, "Good Infection," in *Mere Christianity*. Answer the following questions in response to your reading:

### Chapter 2: **"The Three-Personal God"**

1.     Why is it important that Christians believe in a personal God? What do they mean by this?

2.     How is this Christian idea of a personal God different from the Hindu, Buddhist, or New Age idea that we will be absorbed into God like a drop of water disappearing into the sea?

3. Lewis notes, "In God's dimension, so to speak, you find a being who is three Persons while remaining one Being, just as a cube is six squares while remaining one cube." How might this analogy help someone think about God as three Persons in one?

4. How does Lewis suggest the three Persons of the Trinity are involved in the prayer life of a believer?

5. How does Lewis suggest the Christian definition of the three-personal God came about?

6. What is experiential knowledge?

7. Why does Lewis state that the simple religions are the made-up ones? Do you agree with Lewis?

8.  Why is it necessary for God to reveal Himself to us? How does He reveal Himself to us?

9.  Why is Christian community (what Lewis calls brotherhood) essential to helping us get to know and understand God?

## Chapter 4: "Good Infection"

1.  How can God the Father and God the Son have always existed, yet God the Father be called the source, origin, or cause of God the Son?

2.  How does the New Testament description of the Father and Son relationship help us to understand the nature and character of God?

3.  God is love. If this statement is true, why is it necessary that God have at least two Persons in His one Being?

4. How is the relationship between God the Father, God the Son, and God the Holy Spirit something like a dance or drama?

5. How does the Holy Spirit act through you?

6. How do we share in the life of God and get infected by the life of Christ?

7. According to Lewis, what is the purpose of becoming a Christian?

8. The word Christian means "little Christ." Why is it the goal of the Christian life to become a little Christ?

## Action Steps

1.  Pick one or two of the Scripture passages in this session and meditate upon them daily for a week.

2.  Reflect upon how you would explain the Trinity to a friend. To a stranger.

3.  Commit to praying daily and asking God to show you His truth and wisdom.

## Bible Memory Verses

"And when Jesus was baptized, immediately he went up from the water, and behold, the heavens were opened to him, and he saw the Spirit of God descending like a dove and coming to rest on him; and behold, a voice from heaven said, 'This is my beloved Son, with whom I am well pleased'" (Matthew 3:16–17).

## Concluding Observations on Biblical Passages on the Trinity and Book 4, Chapter 2, "The Three-Personal God," and Chapter 4, "Good Infection," in *Mere Christianity*

The Bible describes the nature and character of God as eternally existing in three Persons, God the Father, God the Son, and God the Holy Spirit. Each Person of the Trinity is fully and equally God and united as one God. Although the word *Trinity* is not in the Bible, it is a word that helps describe the three-in-oneness taught in the Bible from the first chapter of Genesis, where the three Persons of the Trinity were involved in creation, and throughout the Old Testament and New Testament. The teaching of the Trinity is an essential doctrine of the Christian faith; Jesus in His Great Commission commanded the church to make disciples, baptizing them in the name of the Father, Son, and the Holy Spirit. Analogies aren't perfect but can be used to help understand the nature and character of God. Lewis suggests the idea of a cube—six squares united into one cube—and the idea of a loving dance between the three Persons of the Trinity as means of helping us understand the teaching. The idea that God is love affirms that God can't be just one Person, as love assumes more than one actively loving the other. So the Trinity makes sense in that God is able to love because God is three Persons, who love one another actively, yet is one God. Our prayer life may be one of the best means for us to understand how the three Persons of the one God interact with us and help us become "little Christs" or Christians.

**Note:** This study skips book 4, chapter 3, "Time and Beyond Time." In this chapter, Lewis proposes some ideas to answer from a philosophical perspective the question, how can God attend to hundreds of millions of people praying to Him at the same moment in time? Lewis crystallizes the problem being addressed in this question as having to do with *"at the same moment."* Listening to all these people simultaneously reveals a problem in understanding God and His relationship to time and space. Time is chronological, it takes place one second after another and continually moves from past to present to future. Rather than assuming that God always moves from past to future as we do, some theologians, philosophers, and now scientists have promoted the idea that not all things are necessarily bound by time. Lewis's argument is that God is not in time. He is beyond time. He sees past, present, and future all at the same time. God lives in eternity and thus is not hurried. Lewis notes: "He has infinite attention to spare for each one of us." One analogy is that time is an arrow drawn on a piece of paper and God is the piece of paper. God has no history, as He is beyond our reality of time. God foresees our acts yet is outside of time, thus giving us the freedom still to choose what we do. Lewis acknowledges that these ideas are not found in the Bible but are philosophical ways to think about God, time, and space. It can be helpful to some to know that the question posed has possible answers.

# SESSION 3-3

## The Doctrine of Salvation: How to Become a Child of God

*The Son of God became a man to enable men to become sons of God.*

*—C.S. Lewis, Mere Christianity, Book 4, Chapter 5*

## Questions to Explore

1. How did Jesus, the Son of God, become a man?

2. How did Jesus make it possible for a person to be born again of the Spirit?

3. How does a person become a child of God?

## Bible Study

Read John 3:1-21. Answer the following questions based on your reading:

1.  Why do you think Nicodemus, the religious leader, came to Jesus at night?

2.  How did Nicodemus recognize that Jesus had come from God?

3.  How can one see the kingdom of God (enter into heaven)?

4.  How does Jesus explain the idea of being born again?

5.  What does it mean to be born of both water and the spirit?

6.  How does Jesus describe the work of the Holy Spirit in a person's life?

7.    Who is the Son of Man?

8.    Later in the Gospel of John, chapter 19 how will Jesus be lifted up so that everyone who believes may have eternal life?

9.    What does it mean to be given the gift of eternal life? Is that a gift you'd like to have?

10.   Analyze John 3:16 and parse out its meaning phrase by phrase. What does it tell you about God? About how a person can avoid spiritual death?

11.   Who is God's one and only Son? Why is this important to know?

12.   Why did Jesus come to earth?

13.    How can a person receive eternal life?

## Study of *Mere Christianity*

Read book 4, chapter 5, "The Obstinate Toy Soldiers," and chapter 6, "Two Notes," of *Mere Christianity*. Answer the following questions in response to your reading:

## Chapter 5: "The Obstinate Toy Soldiers"

1.    How does Lewis define the natural or created life (*bios*)—what the Bible calls our sinful nature or our flesh?

2.    How does Lewis define the spiritual or begotten life (*zoe*)—what the Bible calls being born of the Spirit or the Spirit-filled life?

3.    Lewis uses the analogy of a tin man being turned into a human being to describe the way Jesus made it possible for human beings to become alive spiritually. Does this analogy help you understand the new life in Christ? Why or why not?

4. Describe all that Jesus did when He, the Second Person of the Trinity, became human Himself. What details does Lewis describe?

5. What difference did Jesus becoming human make to the whole human race?

6. How can we appropriate salvation through Jesus Christ and receive the new life of the Spirit that allows us to enter into new life with Jesus forever?

7. List and discuss other terms or expressions that seek to explain how Jesus Christ has brought the possibility of salvation and a new life in Him to all human beings.

## Chapter 6: "Two Notes"

1. Why did God give human beings free will and the ability to rebel against God?

2. How is the human race like a tree—one huge organism?

3. How is each individual human being tied into the human race? How would you draw a representation of this phenomenon?

4. Lewis suggests that the devil likes to throw us errors in pairs to get us off track. Describe what Lewis means by this.

## Action Steps

1. If you haven't surrendered to Jesus, would you like to do so? If the answer is yes, you can do so now by praying from the heart the following prayer. You may want to pray it out loud along with your study partners.

> Dear God, I confess that I am a sinner. I know that my sin deserves the punishment of death. I believe that Jesus Christ is the Son of God and that He died on the cross for my sins, was buried, and rose again from the dead. I want to turn from my sins and trust Jesus Christ alone as my Savior. Thank You for the forgiveness of my sins and the gift of eternal

life that I can now receive through faith in Jesus' name. Amen.

By confessing with your mouth and believing in your heart that Jesus is Lord, you have now entered into a new life and relationship with Jesus Christ. You are now a disciple of Jesus, on a lifelong journey of love and obedience to your Lord and Savior. It is important for you to share what you have done with a friend, such as the person going through this study with you.

2.    Reflect upon how you would share with a friend how to become a child of God. How would you share the gospel message with a stranger?

3.    Commit to praying daily and asking God to show you His truth and wisdom.

## Bible Memory Verse

"See what kind of love the Father has given to us, that we should be called children of God" (1 John 3:1).

## Concluding Observations on John 3:1-21 and Book 4, Chapter 5, "The Obstinate Toy Soldiers," and Chapter 6, "Two Notes," in *Mere Christianity*

If Adam and Eve in the Garden of Eve hadn't rebelled against God, allowing sin to enter the world, it may be that human beings eventually would have been given eternal life (*zoe*) without the need for a Savior. However, sin did enter the world and the result was that the natural, physical life (*bios*) of human beings became self-centered, sinful, and temporal. We became like "tin soldiers" with corrupted hearts and spiritual lives. The only means for human beings to be reconciled to God, avoid ultimate spiritual death, and receive the gift of eternal life would have to come through a perfect human being who could live and die a sub-stitutionary death on behalf of sinful humanity. Jesus Christ, the Second Person of the Trinity, did just that by being born into the natural world. The Creator of the universe willingly became a fetus in Mary's womb, was born, grew, and lived among us. He came into the world, sent by God the Father out of His deep love for humanity. By living a perfect life, shedding His blood and dying on our behalf, and rising from the dead, He defeated death, sin, and Satan. Jesus made it possible for us to be given eternal life (*zoe*) through Him. He allowed us cold, obstinate tin soldiers to receive new hearts, be born again by the Spirit of God, and enter into new life (*zoe*). Thus we will have been born both of water (*bios*) from our mothers' wombs and then born again of the Spirit (*zoe*). To appropriate this eternal life, we must believe in Jesus Christ, God's only begotten Son, as our Lord and Savior, putting our hope and trust in Him alone. If we don't do this, we will be condemned to perish—the result of our own willful sinfulness and rebellion against God. Lewis summarizes this great truth: "The

Son of God became a man to enable men to become sons of God." This is the Christian doctrine of salvation.

# SESSION 3-4

## The Doctrine of Sanctification–Part 1: How to Become More Like Jesus

*The Christian way is different: harder, and easier. Christ says "Give me All. I don't want so much of your time and so much of your money and so much of your work: I want You. I have not come to torment your natural self, but to kill it . . . I will give you a new self . . . In fact, I will give you Myself: my own will shall become yours."*

*–C.S. Lewis, Mere Christianity, Book 4, Chapter 8*

*The Church exists for nothing else but to draw men into Christ, to make them little Christs. If they are not doing that, all the cathedrals, clergy, missions, sermons, even the Bible itself, are simply a waste of time. God became Man for no other purpose.*

*–C.S. Lewis, Mere Christianity, Book 4, Chapter 8*

*You thought you were going to be made into a decent little cottage: but He is building a palace. He intends to come and live in it Himself.*

*–C.S. Lewis, Mere Christianity, Book 4, Chapter 9*

## Questions to Explore

1.  Once we have been born again, how does our mortal life change?

2.  Is the Christian life easy or difficult?

3.  What is the purpose for the life of the Christian?

4.  How does God work in our lives to make us more like Jesus?

## Bible Study

Read Matthew 16:13-28; Luke 9:23-24. Answer the following questions based on your reading:

1.  Who did some people in Jesus' day think the "Son of Man" was?

2.  Who did Peter say was the promised Messiah, the Christ, the "Son of Man"? How did Peter come up with this answer? Why is this important to know?

3.   What is Jesus' promise about the future of the church? Is His promise coming true? Why or why not?

4.   Why do you think Jesus asked His disciples at this time not to tell anyone?

5.   When Peter heard about Jesus' plan to go to Jerusalem, suffer, die, and rise again on the third day, what was his response? How did Peter come up with this response to Jesus' plans? Why is this important to know?

6.   Beginning in Matthew 16:24, Jesus sets the expectations for His disciples. What does Jesus call His disciples to do?

7.   Are Jesus' demands on the believer's life easy? Why or why not?

8.  Did you previously know that Jesus demands your whole life when you became a new Christian? Describe your previous understanding of Jesus' call on your life.

9.  In a sentence or two, compare the value of the gift of salvation through Jesus with the value of earthly riches. How does knowing the value of Jesus' gift change the way you live?

## Study of *Mere Christianity*

Read book 4, chapter 7, "Let's Pretend," chapter 8, "Is Christianity Hard or Easy?," and chapter 9, "Counting the Cost," in *Mere Christianity*. Answer the following questions in response to your reading:

## Chapter 7: "Let's Pretend"

1.  What does Lewis mean: "that it is like we are pretending when we utter the words in the Lord's Prayer, 'Our Father'"?

2.  How do we "pretend" and dress up as Christ or put on Christ?

3.  How does Christ, the Son of God, turn our "pretense" into a reality by making you or me into a son of God?

4.  How does Christ work on us through our daily routines and practices so that we become more like Him?

5.  How can we help spread the "good infection" of Christ among other people?

6.  Why is it so important that we follow Christ alongside other followers of Jesus?

7. How does the language of the New Testament about believers ("being born again," "putting on Christ," "having the mind of Christ," "being formed") help you understand how you are changed over time to become a "little Christ"?

8. How is a greater understanding of our own sinfulness a sign that Christ is at work in our lives?

9. What does Lewis mean: "After the first few steps in the Christian life we realise that everything which really needs to be done in our souls can be done only by God"?

10. How is it that God does the "pretending" as He begins to see us as "little Christs"?

## Chapter 8: "Is Christianity Hard or Easy?"

1. What is the job of all Christians?

2.  How is the task of all followers of Jesus—to become children of God and to "put on Christ"—different from ordinary ideas of "being good" or "moral"?

3.  Why is it difficult to be moral or good on our own strength and power?

4.  How much does Christ demand from you? How does this make you feel?

5.  How is the Christian life easier than other ways of life? Harder than other ways?

6.  Why does Jesus Christ demand so much from His followers?

7. Where does the real problem come in the Christian's daily life? What comes at you first thing in the morning? How can we learn to live more victoriously first thing in the morning?

8. What habits or disciplines might help us give Jesus our all at the beginning of the day?

9. What does Lewis mean: "The Church exists for nothing else but to draw men into Christ, to make them little Christs. If they are not doing that, all the cathedrals, clergy, missions, sermons, even the Bible itself, are simply a waste of time. God became Man for no other purpose"?

10. Reflect upon the last paragraph of this chapter (8). What do you think of Lewis's concluding observations?

## Chapter 9: "Counting the Cost"

1. What does Jesus mean by "be ye perfect"?

2.   How is our Lord like a dentist?

3.   What did Jesus mean when He said we should "count the cost"?

4.   What did George MacDonald mean when he wrote, "God is easy to please, but hard to satisfy"?

5.   Why should we not be discouraged by God's demand for perfection?

6.   What is God's plan for you as a Christian?

7.   Why should we not be surprised when life becomes rough or difficult as a follower of Jesus?

8. Describe in detail George MacDonald's parable that we are like a house that God is rebuilding.

## Action Steps

1. Commit to starting each morning this week—when everything usually comes flying at you—with five minutes of Scripture reading and prayer—asking the Holy Spirit to fill you and empower you for the day, so you can share the light of Jesus with others. Pray that you might put on Christ, have the mind of Christ, and be a little Christ.

2. Reflect upon the demand of Christ for you to give Him everything. Write out a statement of commitment to Jesus Christ based on Luke 9:23-24. Then put this statement of commitment next to your bedside and read it each morning this month.

3. Commit to praying daily and asking God to show you His truth and wisdom.

## Bible Memory Verses

"And he said to all, 'If anyone would come after me, let him deny himself and take up his cross daily and follow me. For whoever would save his life will lose it, but whoever loses his life for my sake will save it'" (Luke 9:23-24).

## Concluding Observations on Matthew 16:13-28; Luke 9:23-24, and Book 4, Chapters 7, 8, and 9 in *Mere Christianity*

A person who becomes a Christian must read the fine print carefully. Jesus demands nothing less than all of you if you are going to be His disciple. He states in Luke, "If anyone would come after me, let him deny himself and take up his cross daily and follow me." In other words, from the moment you surrender your life to Jesus as your Lord and Savior, you are no longer your own. At the beginning of every day, we are called to "put on Christ" and seek to imitate Him in thought, word, and deed. Our ability to think, speak, and act like Jesus, however, isn't instantaneous; we will be growing in spiritual maturity throughout our lives on earth, only to be finally perfected when we meet Jesus face to face. We must count the cost, be willing to give up earthly minded things, and focus on God's priorities, not our own. This task will not be easy; at times it will be downright difficult and uncomfortable. The good news, however, is that the Helper, the Holy Spirit, will be with us and will empower us as we give Him control to conquer sin in our lives and better represent Jesus to others. Jesus' goal for us is that we will be perfect. This means that He will be rebuilding us into His beautiful temple where the Holy Spirit lives within us. It is important to know that the doctrine of sanctification—the teaching that over time we will become more holy and look more like Jesus as we grow in spiritual maturity—is a reality in the life of the Christian. If we understand it, we won't be surprised when difficulties or trials come our way. We will know how to be filled with the Holy Spirit on a daily basis so that we are given the resources to reflect more brightly the light of Jesus to others and to our world.

# SESSION 3-5

## The Doctrine of Sanctification–Part 2: Becoming New Men and Women in Christ

*Give up yourself, and you will find your real self. Lose your life and you will save it. Submit to death, death of your ambitions and favourite wishes every day and death of your whole body in the end: submit with every fibre of your being, and you will find eternal life. Keep back nothing. Nothing that you have not given away will ever be really yours. Nothing in you that has not died will ever be raised from the dead. Look for yourself, and you will find in the long run only hatred, loneliness, despair, rage, ruin, and decay. But look for Christ and you will find Him, and with Him everything else thrown in.*

–C.S. Lewis, *Mere Christianity, Book 4, Chapter 11*

## Questions to Explore

1.  If Christianity is true, why are some Christians so mean?

2.  How does God change us into "new people"?

3.  What does God demand of us?

4.    Why is just being nice not enough?

## Bible Study

Read Romans 12:1–21. Answer the following questions based on your reading:

1.    What does it mean to offer one's body to God as a "living sacrifice"?

2.    How does God renew our minds so that we no longer think as we did before, but begin to understand His will?

3.    How are we to relate to other people in the church?

4.    What gifts or "graces" does God distribute to Christians for the well-being of the church?

5.    What gifts from God do you think you have?

6.    What verbs does Paul use to describe how the Christian should act and live out his or her new life in Christ?

7.    Describe some examples in which you have seen followers of Jesus living out the Christian life as Paul describes it here.

## Study of *Mere Christianity*

Read book 4, chapter 10, "Nice People or New Men," and chapter 11, "The New Men," in *Mere Christianity*. Answer the following questions in response to your reading:

## Chapter 10: "Nice People or New Men"

1.    If Christianity is true, why are not all Christians obviously nicer than all non-Christians?

2.    Why is it unhelpful to create the general categories *Christians* and *non-Christians* when addressing this question of "niceness"?

3.  Why is it logically possible that a non-Christian might at times be nicer than a Christian?

4.  What does Lewis mean: "The only things we can keep are the things we freely give to God. What we try to keep for ourselves is just what we are sure to lose"?

5.  Why should we not be surprised to find some Christians who are still nasty?

6.  Why does God's redemption always improve people?

7.  How is Christ's work of making new men like the process of turning a horse into a winged creature?

8.  What is God's goal when He turns men and women into sons and daughters of God?

9.  Why does Lewis state that ultimately this question of comparative niceness is merely a means of evading the issues and confronting one's own position when faced with the presence of God?

## Chapter 11: "The New Men"

1.  What does Lewis mean when he argues that Christ's goal is not to improve us but to transform us?

2.  How is Christ the "first instance" of the new man?

3.  What does Lewis mean: "To become new men means losing what we now call 'ourselves.' Out of our selves, into Christ, we must go. His will is to become ours and we are to think His thoughts, to 'have the mind of Christ'"?

4.  What does Lewis mean: "At the beginning I said there were Personalities in God. I will go further now. There are no real personalities anywhere else"?

5.  How can the follower of Jesus Christ give up him- or herself and thus get a real personality from Jesus?

6.  Rewrite the last two sentences of chapter 11 in your own words.

## Action Steps

1.  Daily offer your body to God as a living sacrifice in prayer and ask Him to renew your mind so that you can come to think and act more like Jesus.

2.  Reflect upon your own spiritual gifts. Find ways to use those gifts to bless your Christian friends in the church.

3.  Write down right now some ways in which you can show love, hospitality, and goodness toward the people in your neighborhood, workplace, and family.

4.  Meditate on Romans 12:9-21 this week by reading it daily and praying through it.

5.  Commit to praying daily and asking God to show you His truth and wisdom.

## Bible Memory Verses

"Therefore, if anyone is in Christ, he is a new creation. The old has passed away; behold, the new has come. All this is from God, who through Christ reconciled us to himself and gave us the ministry of reconciliation" (2 Corinthians 5:17-18).

"I have been crucified with Christ. It is no longer I who live, but Christ who lives in me. And the life I now live in the flesh I live by faith in the Son of God, who loved me and gave himself for me" (Galatians 2:20).

## Concluding Observations on Romans 12:1-21 and Book 4, Chapter 10, "Nice People or New Men," and Chapter 11, "The New Men," in *Mere Christianity*

Followers of Jesus are called to surrender all and to give up their bodies as a living sacrifice to God. They are to do so not merely to become good or moral individuals, but rather to become *new persons*. This occurs when we allow Jesus Christ to take over and to live in and through us. When we do this, He begins to change the way we think and act as He renews our minds and empowers us with gifts with which to serve others. He calls us to be active in loving those both inside and outside of the church. We become more hospitable, loving, and caring, and we seek the good and best for others. Jesus doesn't want merely to improve us; He wants to transform us into people who, while maintaining our unique identities, take on His personality, character, and love for God and others. The Christian faith is not about becoming a better person, a nicer person, a moral person, but rather about giving Jesus total control of our lives, of giving up all, and losing all to gain everything in Christ.

# APPENDICES

# APPENDIX 1

## The Apostles' Creed

The Apostles' Creed is not in the Bible, but it was developed by the early church to summarize the apostles' teaching. It is used by historically orthodox Roman Catholic and Protestant churches. It was the creed that C.S. Lewis used as the basis for his understanding of the apostles' teaching that helped shape the themes in book 2 of *Mere Christianity*, "What Christians Believe."

### The Apostles' Creed

I believe in God, the Father almighty,
creator of heaven and earth.
I believe in Jesus Christ, his only Son, our Lord,
who was conceived by the Holy Spirit
and born of the virgin Mary.
He suffered under Pontius Pilate,
was crucified, died, and was buried;
he descended to hell.
The third day he rose again from the dead.
He ascended to heaven
and is seated at the right hand of God the Father almighty.
From there he will come to judge the living and the dead.
I believe in the Holy Spirit,
the holy catholic* church,
the communion of saints,
 the forgiveness of sins,
the resurrection of the body,
and the life everlasting. Amen.

*the universal church made up of all true Christians throughout history

# APPENDIX 2

## A Study of Book 1 of Mere Christianity:
## Right and Wrong as a Clue to the Meaning of the Universe

*If you look for truth, you may find comfort in the end: if you look for comfort you will not get either comfort or truth—only soft soap and wishful thinking to begin with and, in the end, despair. Most of us have got over the pre-war wishful thinking about international politics. It is time we did the same about religion.*

—C.S. Lewis, *Mere Christianity*, Book 1, Chapter 5

### Questions to Explore

1.  Is there such a thing as right and wrong?

2.  Why do cultures around the world have a moral law?

3.  Do human beings live up to their own moral law?

4.  Who is behind the moral law?

5.  Is the moral law a clue to finding meaning in the universe?

## Bible Study

Read Romans 1:16-25. The writer of the book of Romans, the apostle Paul, had a dramatic encounter with the risen Jesus Christ that changed his life forever. He went from being a murderer and persecutor of Christians to being a fully devoted disciple of Jesus. The letter to the Romans lays out some foundational principles about the nature of God, the problems in the world, and the means by which human beings can find hope and salvation through faith in Jesus Christ as Lord and Savior.

Answer the following questions based on your reading of Romans 1:16-25:

1.  Why is Paul not ashamed of the good news (gospel) of Jesus Christ?

2.  How is God described?

3.  How are the "righteous" described? Why is belief or faith in God important?

4.  When and how has God made Himself known to all human beings?

5. Why is it inexcusable not to know that God exists?

6. According to Paul, what have people done who have chosen not to worship God as the Creator and Savior of the world?

7. What are the implications of this passage for men and women in the world today?

Read Romans 2:12-16. Answer the following questions based on your reading:

1. The law of God is made up of all that is known to be right and wrong. How is it that those who know it and those who don't know it are equally declared to be sinful or wrong when they break the law of God?

2. How is it that those who know the law and those who don't know the law are said to be equally good or just when they follow the law of God?

3. How has God revealed the law of God, an understanding of right and wrong, the just and unjust, to all human beings throughout all time and history?

4. What implications does this have?

## Study of *Mere Christianity*

Answer the following questions in response to your reading:

Read book 1, chapter 1, "The Law of Human Nature," in *Mere Christianity*.

1. What is the law of nature?

2. Although different cultures may have varying moralities, how are all moralities of the world alike?

3. How can you prove that all people believe in some form of right and wrong?

4. What are the two main points that Lewis makes in this chapter?

Read book 1, chapter 2, "Some Objections," in *Mere Christianity*.

1. How is the moral law different from instinct?

2. How is moral law different from social convention?

3. How is the moral law like mathematics?

4.    Summarize Lewis's main points in this chapter.

Read book 1, chapter 3, "The Reality of the Law," in *Mere Christianity*

1.    What is the difference between "laws of nature," such as the law of gravity, and "the law of human nature" or the moral law?

2.    What is the difference between how human beings ought to behave and how they behave? Why is this important to note?

3.    Why does Lewis conclude that "the law of human nature" or "the law of right and wrong" must be a *real* thing that is not made up by ourselves?

4.   Summarize Lewis's main points in this chapter.

Read book 1, chapter 4, "What Lies behind the Law," in *Mere Christianity*.

1.   What is the materialist's perspective on the nature of the universe?

2.   What is the religious perspective on the nature of the universe?

3.   What does "the law of human nature" or the moral law teach us about the nature of the universe?

4.   Why might we conclude that a directing power behind the universe has set up a moral order that we are compelled to follow yet do so imperfectly?

5.    Summarize Lewis's main points in this chapter.

Read book 1, chapter 5, "We Have Cause to Be Uneasy," in *Mere Christianity*.

1.    Why is it more important to be on the right road than to be making "progress"?

2.    How is the created universe a possible clue to knowing about the One who created it?

3.    How is the moral law a clue to knowing about the One who has put the moral law in our conscience?

4.    How is goodness either the great safety or the great danger?

5.   What are the basic claims of Christianity?

6.   Summarize Lewis's main points in this chapter.

## Action Steps

1.   Summarize the line of thought in book 1, "Right and Wrong as a Clue to the Meaning of the Universe," in eight or fewer sentences.

2.   Share this line of thought or argument for the existence of God with a friend. Discuss and determine if it makes sense.

3.   Pray and ask God to give you an opportunity this month to share your faith with someone who is seeking for truth.

## Bible Memory Verses

"For what can be known about God is plain to them, because God has shown it to them. For his invisible attributes, namely, his eternal power and divine nature, have been clearly perceived, ever since the creation of the world, in the things that have been made. So they are without excuse" (Romans 1:19-20).

"For when Gentiles, who do not have the law, by nature do what the law requires, they are a law to themselves, even though they do not have the law. They show that the work of the law is written on their hearts, while their conscience also bears witness, and their conflicting thoughts accuse or even excuse them on that day when, according to my gospel, God judges the secrets of men by Christ Jesus" (Romans 2:14-16).

## Concluding Observations on Romans 1:16-25; 2:12-16 and Book 1 of *Mere Christianity*

The beauty, order, and majesty of the created world in nature points to a Divine Creator. As Psalm 19:1 says, "The heavens declare the glory of God"; in so doing, nature suggests that someone greater than ourselves is behind the origins of the universe and the world as we know it.

Likewise, every man and woman carries a conscience that bears witness to the idea that some things are right and some things are wrong. In other words, there is a moral law that stands outside of us and can be found in all cultures, times, and places in human history. This moral or natural law points to the possibility of Something or Someone who is directing the universe. It is like a Mind or a Person that is urging us to do right and makes us feel responsible and guilty when we do wrong. The moral or natural law and the grandeur of nature are clues to the meaning of the universe that point us to the idea that there is a Creator who has instilled within us a sense of right and wrong.

Christianity believes that there is a moral law and that behind that moral law is a Power. When people break the moral law, they put themselves wrong with the Power. The result is that people are in need of someone to make things right again for them, as they are unable to get right with the Power or God themselves. This makes Christianity an uncomfortable faith and idea—that human beings are at odds with the Creator of the world and the One behind the moral law.

On the other hand, Christianity is comforting as God, in His love for humanity, sent His Son, to become a man to save men and women from their broken relationship with God. He makes it possible for us to be forgiven and receive an unspeakable comfort. If this is remotely possible, it is imperative that men and women explore this idea seriously, seeking truth and reality, not merely basking in wishful thinking.

# APPENDIX 3

## Facilitator/Leader Guide

## What Approach?

### *One-on-One Discipleship or the Triad/Quad Approach*

Probably the most effective use of this discipleship training program would be through a one-on-one approach or with a small group of three to four people (a triad or quad). In most cases, it is best to have one person serve as the leader or group facilitator, usually the more mature believer. However, the program is set up so a group of peers could go through the program and share the leadership throughout the study.

### *Small Groups*

Another method would be to use this resource with a small group. In this case, the facilitator should ensure that everyone in the group is engaged, has the opportunity to participate, and is receiving the encouragement and exhortation needed to get the most out of the study.

### *Plan Well*

**P-L-A-N:** Before you begin, take time to plan by reading this leadership guide and the study guide introduction. Then begin the steps of planning:

**P–Purpose:** Know the purpose of the *Discipleship with C.S. Lewis* program—that you and your friends will experience authentic spiritual growth as you seek to learn how to become more mature disciples of Jesus Christ. Determine how you can best communicate the purpose of this discipleship program to the people you are going to invite to participate.

**L–Logistics:** Determine the logistics of:

> **When:** When will you meet (date, time, for how long)?

> **Where:** Where will you meet (home, church, workplace)?

> **What:** What will you need to do to prepare the place for the weekly meetings (seating, lighting, room temperature, beverages, snacks, childcare, removal of distractions)?

> **Who:** Who will take care of the various planning pieces? Don't be afraid to delegate. People like to contribute and actually become more committed when they play a role in the group, even if it's just preparing refreshments or setting up chairs.

Possible roles for a small group include:

> Leader

> Assistant Leader

> Hospitality Coordinator

> Childcare Coordinator

Facilities Coordinator

**A–Activities:** The *Discipleship with C.S. Lewis* program has a suggested activity plan for different types of groups. If you have time to meet for a meal, or even dessert, the fellowship over food can help build the relationships and thus enhance the overall experience. Below are a few suggested formats. The 90- to 120-minute weekly sessions are the ideal. If time is of the essence, a 60-minute session can be used, although it restricts group discussion.

## Sample for One-on-One, Triad, Quad, or Small-Group Study Activities

(Total: 90 minutes)

| | |
|---|---|
| 10 minutes: | Social Time |
| 5 minutes: | Introduction of Topic and Prayer |
| 30 minutes | Discuss Bible Study Questions |
| 30 minutes: | Discuss *Mere Christianity* Questions & Action Steps |
| 15 minutes | Closing: Recite Memory Verse & Prayer Time |

## Dinner and Study Model

(Total: 120 minutes)

| | |
|---|---|
| 40 minutes: | Simple Dinner and Social Time (pizza, salad, drinks and desserts or a potluck) |
| 5 minutes: | Introduction of Topic and Prayer |
| 30 minutes | Discuss Bible Study Questions |

| 30 minutes: | Discuss *Mere Christianity* Questions & Action Steps |
| 15 minutes | Closing: Recite Memory Verse & Prayer Time |

## Sunday School Class or Workplace Model

(Total: 60 minutes)

| 5 minutes | Introduction of Topic and Prayer |
| 20 minutes | Discuss Bible Study Questions |
| 20 minutes: | Discuss *Mere Christianity* Questions & Action Steps |
| 15 minutes: | Closing: Recite Memory Verse & Prayer Time |

Take time each week to plan out the meeting activities, so things flow smoothly. **Always start and end on time**. People will get discouraged if the meetings extend beyond the announced time or start late. If you desire, you can end the formal meeting on time and give people the option to stay later to fellowship, pray, and talk. But always give people the opportunity to end at the scheduled times.

**N–Needs:** Be attuned to the needs of the participants. As you pray for the Holy Spirit to guide your planning process, He will help you determine the needs of your particular group and what your responsibilities are in meeting those needs.

In his book *Destination Community,* Rick Howerton suggests some key questions to pray about as you prepare for each meeting:

Is there:     Someone to pray with?

Someone needing counsel?

Someone to encourage?

Someone to hold accountable?

Something to celebrate
with someone?

Something to learn?

A need to be met?

A call to be made?

A conflict to be resolved?

## Pray about and Recruit Participants

The second task of the leader is to pray about and recruit the participants. Ask the Lord to lead you to the right people. Who can benefit from participating in the study? Then begin inviting secular friends and neighbors, or others who know Christ and might like to learn more. Don't be disappointed if some say, "No, thank you." Persevere and keep on inviting until you get a committed small group together.

Jim Collins, author of the modern leadership best seller *Good to Great*, notes, "Great endeavors are accomplished best when the right people are in the right place doing the right thing." As you pray and ask for His will regarding the make-up of group, He can arrange the right people in the right place doing the right thing.

A personal invitation or a phone call is the preferred method of communication; an impersonal e-mail might be overlooked or missed.

Bobb Biehl uses the following saying in his book *Mentoring*: "Don't hesitate—initiate."

Here are some questions you should be prepared to answer when recruiting participants. Try to formulate an answer that would satisfy you as a potential participant.

Be prepared to answer the following questions when recruiting a potential disciple:

1.  How much time each week will it take for me to prepare for and do the study?

2.  How long will the study last—how many weeks, how many hours per session?

3.  What kind of homework is involved?

4.  Does it cost anything?

5.  Do you have to know a lot of Bible or be able to pray out loud to be in the group?

6.  How many people will be in the group?

7.  What are we going to do in the meetings?

8.  Who else is coming?

9.  Do you provide childcare?

10. Can I leave midway through the study if I find it's just not for me?

## Group Size

It is recommended that discussion groups include no more than six people including the discussion facilitator. It is hard to have interactive discussions with groups larger than six. If you have recruited a large group, break up into smaller groups for the discussion time.

## Develop a Group Covenant

Covenants provide a means of providing purpose, balance, and accountability within small-group relationships. If people have knowingly signed a covenant, they are more likely to follow-through on their commitment. As well, the covenant makes it easier for people to give grace and/or lovingly confront someone who is not living up to the covenant.

For example, if someone is regularly missing the group's meetings, the leader of the group can say, "Hey, we've missed you recently. Your contribution to the group is important and necessary for our group to function and grow. What can we do to help you make it to the session next week and fulfill your covenant?"

An agreed-upon covenant needs to take into consideration both the principles and logistics needed to achieve the group's goal. It would be wise to write up your covenant and then distribute copies to everyone in the group. Have the group discuss it and express any concerns or reservations. It can be adapted to meet the needs of the group as long as it doesn't compromise the mission of the program. Key components might include:

- **Attendance:** a commitment to attend the weekly meetings barring an unexpected emergency.

- **Preparation:** a commitment to do the homework and come prepared to the meetings. However, someone who hasn't finished the homework should be encouraged to come anyway so he or she can benefit from the group's discussion and get back on track.

- **Prayer:** a commitment to pray for the group, that the Holy Spirit would help everyone grow spiritually through all the components.

- **Confidentiality:** anything shared in the group must stay in the group and not be shared with others. This is an important part of the covenant, as it builds trust when maintained and allows people to be more open.

- **Openness:** a willingness to share and participate in the discussions.

- **Honesty:** a commitment to being honest and forthright in all relationships within the group.

- **Sensitivity:** a commitment to being sensitive to the needs of others in the group.

- **Love:** a commitment to love those in the group as commanded by Christ Himself.

## Facilitate Discussion

The great thing about this study program is that you don't have to be a theologian or biblical scholar to lead it. You need to be (1) a committed follower of Jesus Christ, who (2) wants to grow spiritually and (3) wants to bring people alongside to grow. Most of the programming is already done for you. However, you will be asked to facilitate the group discussion. You can use the questions from the study to help do this. These questions can be adopted, adapted, or you can use some questions of your own to get people talking. The key is to get others talking rather than doing the talking yourself.

An ask-don't-tell policy is a good approach when leading the discussion around the theme of the week. People should be ready to talk, assuming they have done the Bible study and reading in *Mere Christianity* before coming.

Some things to remember:

- Remember the questions, who?, what?, when?, where?, why?, and how?

- Give people time to answer. Don't answer your own question. Rephrase it if you'd like, but don't be afraid of "pregnant pauses." Someone might be ready to birth an amazing response, but it takes time sometimes.

- Be affirming by using expressions such as great insight; you're on the right track; can you expand on that?; wow!

- Repeat responses as a way to get people to continue talking.

- Don't ask yes/no questions. If you do, have people expand their answers.

- Redirect people if they start to get off track. It's all right to politely interrupt and ask them to get back to the question or the main idea of the conversation.

- Don't go off on rabbit trails—topics outside of the focus of the meeting.

- Don't let one person dominate the conversation. Politely ask to hear from others in the group.

## Start and End on Time

This point was stated earlier, but it is crucial to maintaining the morale of your group. If you meet the expectations of your group when it comes to the beginning and ending time of your meeting, you'll be trusted with other things later on. Be trustworthy in the little things such as timing, and people will begin to trust you on more important matters. People live busy lives and need to know that they'll be dismissed on time. If you extend beyond the scheduled closing, you may lose people in future meetings. As well, start on time so people show up on time. If you begin starting late, people will begin arriving late. It's just human nature.

## Model What It Takes to Grow from the Study

Prepare each week for the group study. In other words, practice what you preach and complete the Bible study, reading in *Mere Christianity*, and memory verse prior to each session.

## Pray and Enjoy the Program!

Pray for the members of your group and pray that the Holy Spirit would guide the discussion. Pray that all distractions would be removed during the meeting. Do the work, show up to the group meeting, facilitate the discussion, get to know the participants, and enjoy the program!